BEGINNER'S GUIDE TO SQUASH

Beginner's Guide to Squash

Richard Hawkey

PELHAM BOOKS

First published in Great Britain by
PELHAM BOOKS LTD
52 *Bedford Square*
London WC I
1973
© 1973 *Richard Hawkey*

ISBN 0 7207 0682 3

Set and Printed in Great Britain by
Tonbridge Printers Ltd, Peach Hall Works, Tonbridge, Kent
in Baskerville eleven on thirteen point on paper supplied by
P. F. Bingham Ltd, and bound by James Burn
at Esher, Surrey

Contents

Acknowledgements

The author would like to express his very sincere thanks to Alison Brailsford and David Bernard for their help with the photographs, and to Karen Gardner for her hard work with the typewriter.

Illustrations

LINE DRAWINGS

Introduction

It is a very rare phenomenon when a game, which has been in existence over a hundred years, suddenly begins to expand in an enormous world-wide boom, and becomes a headline-making international sport. This is what happened, and indeed is still happening, to squash. There are obviously a number of contributory factors, but equally obviously, it must be a fact that squash is the game that fits in best with modern life. Were it not so, such a vast and rapid development could never have happened, and thousands, even millions, of people, who a few years ago thought that squash was a drink, a vegetable or a crowd, now pay considerable sums to run around a court fairly regularly. Why?

In England, perhaps the first consideration is the weather. When the ground is frozen too hard for rugger, or it is too soft and muddy for hockey, and fog has cancelled soccer, it is still possible to play squash. In summer, when the tennis courts are awash, and bad light has stopped play at Lord's, the squash courts still beckon. And of course it is useful to be able to get one's exercise somehow, when the game one intended to play has had to be cancelled.

Time too, has an effect in a couple of ways. It is never very satisfactory trying to play golf or cricket after dark, and it is still comparatively rare, in ordinary members' clubs, to have floodlights for the other outdoor sports. But squash is available at the switching on of a light. This means that people, whose work or studies require them to keep unusual hours, can have a game, whenever their free time happens to be.

And as squash is such a concentrated form of exercise, it means that a person with only a lunch hour to spare, or an hour before going out in the evening or before going to bed, can get all the physical training he needs or wishes at these times. Perhaps this is the most important way in which squash suits our modern way of life.

Then there is the question of expense. Although the game is now far more commercial than it was, and many centres are now in it for profit, as opposed to the old members' clubs run for the benefit of those who belonged, it is still a very cheap game to play. You only need one racket, as against a whole set of golf clubs; the racket itself is cheaper than a tennis racket, and you need only one ball, instead of a box of six! Subscriptions and court fees compare favourably with other sports, and one does not need any special clothing like studded boots, batting gloves or tin hats. All one needs is tennis type clothing, preferably white, and shoes, the one proviso being that the soles of the shoes must not be black, as this marks the light wood of the court floors. When one reaches the stage of playing matches, white clothing is required by the rules, but there is no need for the beginner to go to the expense of buying this, until he or she decides to take up the game properly.

There are many excellent games, which mainly flourish at schools and universities, but which are 'dead ends', simply because they are not played widely enough for people to continue playing, after leaving the educational establishments behind. Such games are rackets, real tennis (as opposed to lawn of that ilk) and the various codes of fives. Unless a devotee of one of these games is very lucky, it is improbable that his business will enable him to live near enough to a club, or even a court, where he can continue to play. Squash nowadays is spreading so rapidly, that the converse is true; a keen squash player would have to be incredibly unlucky to be sent anywhere more than half an hour's journey at the most from the nearest club. The same argument prevails, if one is sent abroad. The game is already at 'boom' level in Australia, New Zealand and South Africa; there are courts in most other parts of Africa, in India, Pakistan and Egypt; and with Sweden leading the way, courts are springing up in northern Europe, in countries like Finland and Germany, while Denmark, Holland and Belgium have always been interested. Across the Atlantic, there are many courts in the U.S.A. and Canada, although the game is a bit different, for reasons that I will explain when we discuss the history of the game. Even Japan has now caught the bug and reputedly thousands of courts are going up there. So, unless your job is going to take you to Tristan da Cunha or Greenland, the odds are that you will find it possible to continue playing squash.

I have already said that squash is a concentrated form of exercise, and as such it has become increasingly popular with players of other sports, such as rugger and soccer, for keeping fit between matches. It is rather more enjoyable than running round the block, or even working out in a gym, and it not only increases stamina, but also improves agility, speed and quickness of thought and reaction, and as we said before, a very satisfactory training session can be crammed into half an hour on court.

Another advantage of squash is that one does not need to wait for a whole team of eleven or fifteen to be gathered together before a game can be played. All that is necessary is one other player, not necessarily of the same standard, and if there is simply nobody available, one person on his own can have a very useful and energetic half hour.

For the ambitious young player, there is an ever-increasing number of tournaments every week and week-end, which he can enter, and innumerable club and county tournaments for him to take part in, either as an individual or as a member of a team. Very attractive rewards, in the shape of considerable prize money, tours abroad and so on, encourage the talented youngster to practise, to train and to think about the game.

Perhaps the greatest attraction squash has for the beginner is that it is one of the easiest games of all to start. Just about everyone, at some stage of their childhood, hit a ball up against a wall with some form of implement. This is basically what squash is, and where one begins. Thus, most people can 'get off the ground' at Squash in their first practice session, and in no time at all are able to have enjoyable rallies and a good deal of exercise, whether or not they know the rules at this stage, or are making their own up as they go along.

Another thing in favour of squash is that it is a very sociable game. Not only do members of the fair sex play it and play it well, but even if they only go along to spectate, a modern squash club is a pleasant and comfortable place to visit, and most of them have a lively social side to them. And of course the game itself is not too long and dreary for even the most unsportsminded female to sit through!

I suppose the final point I want to make is the most important. However reasonable all the previous arguments in favour of playing squash may have been, people would not be queuing up for court space all over the country, and indeed the world, simply because it was good for them, or a logical choice of recreation, or even cheap. All these things are true, and are reasons why the expansion in the game is so fast and so widespread. But the basic reason behind the continued existence of the sport and its development, is that it is a thoroughly good game to play. If people did not enjoy playing it, they might try it once and then give up, or play for a while, because they needed to keep fit for something else, or play occasionally when the weather prevented their usual form of exercise. They certainly would not get 'bitten' by the game to such an extent that new courts and new clubs are springing up like mushrooms, and however many more appear on the scene, it seems to make no difference to the difficulty of actually booking a court. No, people are clamouring for court space because they enjoy playing immensely; some are ambitious and want to improve, others are happy to trot round and try to lighten the 'stockbroker belt'. All play seriously and feel better for playing, if for no other reason than that it has worked up a marvellous thirst! So, for whatever reason seems the most relevant to you and your own particular circumstances, come and have a go at squash. I am pretty sure you will want to come again . . . and again . . . and again!

1. The Basics of Squash

Before actually going to the expense and trouble of buying a racket, it would be sensible to go along and have a look at a game of squash in progress. At first, it probably looks a mad, noisy, scrambling affair, and if you do not know what the game is all about, it must be very confusing.

THE COURT – AND HOW A RALLY IS PLAYED

Perhaps the easiest way to understand what is happening is to realise that basically squash is the same as the game of lawn tennis, which everyone has seen, at least on television, and most have played. In tennis someone serves a ball to his opponent, and provided it is a correct service, and the other person returns it correctly, a rally is in progress, and continues until one of the players fails to hit the ball before it has bounced twice on the floor, hits it into the net or hits it out of court. It is exactly the same at squash. The only thing that is different is that there is now a high wall across where the net normally is, and instead of hitting the ball over the net to one's opponent on the other side of it, one now hits the ball above the squash equivalent of the net, against this 'front' wall, so that it rebounds and the opponent plays his stroke from the same area. The rest is just as in tennis; one of the players serves, the other returns, and the rally continues until one player fails to hit it before it bounces twice, hits it too low against the wall (into the net, so to speak), or hits it out.

Then we come to the differences! Not only has a wall been

built across where the net normally is, but also down the inside tram lines and across the base line, so that a squash court
is in fact a four-walled room. During a rally, the ball may
hit one or more of these walls, either as the player intends, or
as a result of a mishit, as long as the ball does not touch the
floor between being struck by the player's racket and striking
the front wall correctly, and as long as it does not bounce
on the floor for the second time on its return from the front
wall before the other player hits it. In passing, it is perhaps
worth pointing out that these other walls are one of the main
reasons why squash is an easier game for beginners than
tennis. In tennis, any mishit, or even any slightly misdirected
stroke, will go flying out over the side lines or the base line.
In squash, they rebound into play, and the rally continues!

Let us now have a look at the court, or at the diagram of
the court. First of all, look at the front wall, the one against
which every correct shot is struck. At the foot of it, there is
the 'tin', with a board, painted red, on top of it. This is the
equivalent to the net at tennis, and any ball striking this tin
or board, or indeed failing to reach it, is 'down' and the rally
is ended. Unlike tennis, a ball striking the top of the board,
and going on to hit the front wall is still down; there is no
equivalent to the 'net cord' shot, which counts as a good return. This board is only 19 inches off the ground, so is a good
deal lower than the net, but it does not seem any easier to
avoid! At the top of the front wall, 15 feet above the floor,
there is a red line; this line joins sloping lines down the side
walls, which join up with a line 7 feet above the floor across
the back wall, and these four are the 'out of court' lines.
When the ball hits any of these lines, or the walls above them,
or anything in the roof, it is 'out'. Note that I said it was
'out' when a ball actually hits a line, and you must remember
that in squash, again unlike tennis, the lines are wrong, just
as a ball hitting the board is down, as I have just explained.
One other point: a ball can go as high above the out of
court lines as the roof of the court allows, provided it does not

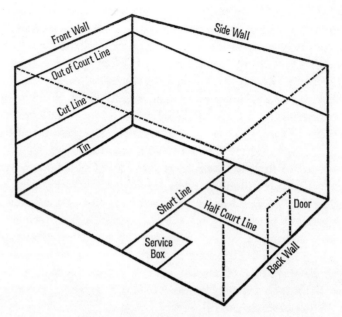

FIG. 1. The Court

actually touch anything, and still be in play; it is only out when it does actually touch a wall, or a light, and so on. The line across the middle of the front wall and all the lines on the floor are only there for the service, and once the ball is correctly in play, are forgotten for the rest of the rally, so I will explain all about them when we come to discuss the service in a little while.

SAFETY, AND CLOTHING

Before I go on to explain how a squash match is scored, and the various more complicated rules, I would like to say one or two very important things about safety. In tennis, badminton, real tennis and table tennis, your opponent is the other side of the court, separated from you by a net, and however clumsy a mover you are, or however wide a racket swing you may take, you are not endangering his or her life in any way. In squash, your opponent has been brought round to the same side of the net as you, and any wild swing, or physical awkwardness can easily result in quite serious injury. One of the problems is that, often, players come to squash via other games, with Tennis as the most frequent 'culprit'. With a heavy racket and a heavy ball, a full swing of the arm is necessary at 'Wimbledon' – but it can open up a series of very nasty cuts on a squash court! Because of the physical proximity of the two players, there are complex rules, as we shall see later, to cover cases of obstruction, and these rules force the players, as far as possible, to keep out of each other's way. Always remember to stop and ask for a 'let', that is to say, to start the rally again, if you feel there is any danger of hitting your opponent with your racket, running into him, tripping him up, or in any way injuring him. Even hitting him with the ball can be painful, and if you happen to get him in the eye, it can be very dangerous, so do be extremely careful.

The main risk of injury comes when players are beginning to play; they have not yet learned how best to position themselves and to move round the court out of each other's way, and nor have they acquired accuracy with their own shots, so that these are played into 'open' parts of the court. Also, in their initial enthusiasm, they probably try to hit too hard, have not yet learned how to use the wrist properly, and so are taking a full scything sweep with the full arm. It is essential then, right from the very start, to bear the need for safety very much in mind.

Similarly, you will be very unpopular with the court owner or club committee if you go on court in black-soled shoes. These leave 'skid marks' all over the floor, which are very difficult to clean off; not only does it eventually make for a very dark floor, against which it is difficult to see the dark ball, but also the lines these skids leave are unsightly, and it is difficult to time strokes when the ball is approaching across a mottled surface. Apart from this, you can wear any suitable

clothing consistent with the laws of decency and the temperature in the court! If you start playing in matches, you will
be required to wear all white, but to start with, be comfortable, and begin worrying about the clothing regulations
when your play has developed to the point, where the club
team can deprive itself of your services no longer!

SCORING

So far I have explained how a rally is played, but have not
yet described the way in which the scoring works in squash.
It is normal for a match to consist of the best of five games,
just as tennis consists of the best of five sets. A game in squash
is won by the first player to reach nine points, unless the
score reaches 'Eight all', and a point is scored when the
person, who is serving, wins the rally. If the rally is won by
the receiver of the service, the score remains the same, but he
gains the service, and of course, with it the right to score a
point, if he wins the next rally. A player, having once won
the service, continues to serve until he loses a rally, scoring
a point each time he wins one. Thus, a match which a player
wins 9-0 9-0 9-0 could be over in 27 rallies, but if the
service has changed frequently, a game which ends 9-0, and
is apparently very one-sided, could in fact be won by 54
rallies to 45!

It is probably helpful now to introduce some of the
generally accepted terminology of squash, in order to make
further explanations more clear. The person serving at squash
is known as 'Hand in' and the receiver as 'Hand out'. A
'Hand' is the term used for a series of points, in which the
same 'Hand in' continued to serve. Thus, one can say that a
player won four points in his first hand, or there were eight
blank hands, as each player in turn hit winners off the
opponent's service. You will learn later, when we come to
discuss the duties of the Marker, who is the person, who
calls out the score, that he always calls the server's, i.e. Hand
in's, score first. This might be 3-2, and if Hand out were to

win that rally, the score would remain the same, but would now be called 2–3, and to indicate this, he precedes the call with the words 'Hand out', so this expression not only refers to the person who is receiving the service in a particular rally, but also to the situation that occurs when that person wins the rally, and takes over the service.

Now we must explain what happens when the score reaches 8 all. For this to occur, Hand in must have served with the score at 7–8, and have won the rally. At that moment, the score is 8 all, and Hand out must choose one of two things. He must either say 'No set' or 'Set two'. If he elects 'No Set', the game continues, as before, to 9, and one of the players wins it by 9–8. If he picks 'Set two', which is far more frequent, it gives him rather more chance of recovering the service, and saves him from losing the game by 'sudden death' – the loss of just one rally; the game then continues to 10, and one of the players will win it 10–9 or 10–8.

It will sometimes happen, for example in the early rounds of a crowded tournament, that something less than the best of five games will be played, and any club may make what regulations it wishes for its own competitions.

THE AMERICAN AND DOUBLES GAMES

In America, where the game is slightly different, the scoring is also slightly different. There, each rally counts a point, whether it is won by Hand in or Hand out, and the game continues to 15, with similar choices for Hand out as in our 8 all situation, when the score reaches 13 all or 14 all, provided it has not been 13 all previously. At 13 all, he may elect 'Set 5', and the game continues until one player has won 18 points, or 'Set 3', which is up to 16, or 'No Set', which leaves the game as it was, to be won by the first player to reach 15. At 14 all, provided one of these choices has not already been made at 13 all, Hand out may choose 'Set 3', in which case the game continues to 17, or 'No set', in which case the next rally decides the game, and one player wins it 15–14.

It is useful to note this method of scoring, partly because there is a movement afoot to bring the two games closer together, and one of the suggestions is that we should adopt the American scoring system, which in any case, is the system used in our doubles game. Officially, doubles should be played in a larger court than the normal singles one, with a hard ball and stronger racket, which are the normal implements of the American game, but there is only one doubles court in the country, as far as I know, at the moment, and this is in Edinburgh. However, some very enjoyable social doubles can be enjoyed with our balls and rackets in our normal singles courts, and some tournaments even include doubles events. It would not be possible to make these serious championships, because with four bodies and rackets in the limited space of a court, there has to be a great deal of give and take to avoid continual collisions and the risk of injury. If too much hung on the game, this might no longer be the case.

2. *Starting to Play*

I hope now that a beginner has been persuaded to take up squash, and has understood enough about how the game works to be able to follow a match, which is in progress. It is now time for him (or her!) to start playing. Before we can discuss the pros and cons of the various strokes, and how, why, and when to play them, the beginner must first learn the knack of hitting the ball with the racket, roughly in the direction that is intended. Obviously, the ultimate aim is to be able, at will, to place the ball into the part of the court where your opponent least wants it placed. This may involve hitting it very hard or very softly, taking it early or just before it bounces for the second time, hitting it high or low, hitting it directly on to the front wall or playing it deliberately against a side wall, hitting it straight up and down the court, or playing it across court.

STANCE, GRIP AND STROKES

We shall discuss the various strokes and how to use them later, but what a beginner must realise from the start is that there is this very wide range of possible shots in squash, a far greater range than in tennis, for example, because of the side walls. He must also realise that rallies in squash are much longer than in other games, because it is more difficult to hit a winner in the limited space of a court, where the front wall takes much of the pace off a hard-hit shot. It follows, therefore, that pure brute force is not enough in squash, and some subtlety is called for in order to wrongfoot and deceive an opponent. This is best achieved by use of the wrist, but to make anticipation of the shot as difficult as possible, a player should play each stroke from the same basic position and with the same swing of the racket.

The point I am trying to make is that it does matter from the start what sort of stance a player adopts, and the type of racket swing he develops. Of course, there will be many occasions, in a fast game, when a player will have no time to get into a set position, but these will be the moments when he is doing not much more than playing a defensive stroke. If he waits, he will get the chance to play a deliberate stroke while he is on balance, and that is when he can play any one of his repertoire, and hope to deceive his opponent.

Ideally, this position is with the player facing the side wall nearest to him, whether on his forehand or backhand half of the court, with the front foot rather nearer that wall than is the back foot, aiming to strike the ball as it is roughly level with the front foot, and between it and the side wall. In order to allow the wrist to be brought into play, the ball should be far enough away from the body for the arm and racket to be more nearly horizontal than vertical, and as the stroke is played the player's weight should be transferred on to the front foot.

The racket should start its swing in a 'cocked' position; this means it should be held with its head high, by means of the wrist, and whipped through, and the follow through should again bring the head up, and not round in a wide arc, where it would be liable to decapitate an opponent. To do this, a reasonably orthodox grip should be aimed at. I say 'reasonably' orthodox, because there have been minor variations among the top players, and if a pupil of mine had a slightly unusual grip, but was still able to play any of the shots consistently well, and did not need to change the grip at all for any of them, I would not interfere. The orthodox grip itself can most easily be obtained by holding the racket out horizontally in front of you, with the non-racket hand, and with the head of the racket vertical, and by then 'shaking hands' with the handle. Obviously, each player's grip must be comfortable for him, and he must decide how near the end of the handle, or how far up it, he is going to hold it. What is important is that whatever grip he does choose will enable him to play any shot, forehand or backhand, without changing the position of his hand; there just is not time for this at squash.

THE RACKET

Now perhaps might be the moment to say a little about the racket. There are a wide range of these, at considerably varying prices. I have always felt that it is false economy on the part of a beginner to buy a really cheap racket; once he is sure he wants to carry on playing it is much better to invest in a good racket, which is much more likely to stand up to the banging on the wall that any beginner is bound to inflict on it, while he is getting used to the bounce of a squash ball. Breaking three £4 rackets is a lot more expensive than not breaking one £7 racket!

As far as the weight of a racket is concerned, this is a relatively unimportant matter in squash, as all rackets are relatively light and easy to wield. Obviously some are lighter than others, and very young players for example, or ladies with less strong wrists, should choose a light racket. The different 'feel' of a squash racket is more in its balance than in its actual weight, and it is a matter of personal preference whether one prefers a racket with a little more, or less, weight in the head. It is, of course, sensible to get used to a particular type of racket and stick to it throughout one's squash career. As a beginner will find, when he has been playing for a little time, accuracy depends very much on a player's 'touch', and having to use a racket one is not accustomed to can make all the difference between playing a winning shot and hitting the tin!

One warning note I would like to sound is to advise against

buying rackets with steel, or some other substance, in the shaft. A completely wooden framed racket, made in one piece, must be stronger than one with joins in it; when the racket strikes a wall, it is less likely to break if the whole length of it can 'give' and take up the strain, than if part of the shaft is more rigid, and the same strain has to be taken up by less racket. You will no doubt notice how often these other rackets break at the shoulder, where the join is, and there is always the danger of the head of the racket flying off and injuring an opponent or spectator.

THE BALL

The other essential for the beginner is, of course, a ball. A squash ball is a piece of rubbery material surrounding some air, and the bounce of the ball, that is to say, how high it will rise from the floor and how far it will rebound from a wall, is dependent on two things. One is the actual consistency of the fabric of the ball, and its thickness, and the other is the temperature of the air inside the ball. Air expands as it warms up, and so, whether the air is heated by the friction caused by repeated severe blows from a racket, or simply because it is in a hot place, once the air becomes warm, the ball becomes more 'bouncy'. Obviously, it is in a beginner's interest to use a ball which is bouncing fairly high of its own accord, because initially he will not be hitting it hard or often enough to create the frictional heat necessary to warm it up, and yet will need a ball which gives him some chance of getting to, despite his lack of anticipation at this stage.

With this, and the range of temperatures which one encounters in squash courts, in mind, the manufacturers produce, and the Associations approve, four speeds of ball. These are identifiable by a coloured dot, which is either yellow, white, red or blue. These are in order of increasing speed; a ball is said to be 'slow' or 'fast', depending on whether it bounces low or high respectively, thus giving slow or fast rallies, and thus the yellow dot ball is the slowest and the blue dot the fastest.

Initially, especially if he is playing on a cold court, and not a centrally-heated one, a beginner would be wise to get hold of a red or blue dot, and not be influenced by the fact that the top tournaments insist on a yellow dot. These championships are usually held in centrally-heated clubs, and obviously the players entering for them are experienced and talented, and will be able to heat the ball up rapidly. To use anything but the slowest available ball for them would make for interminable rallies, because they would find it impossible to put the high-bouncing ball out of their opponent's reach.

EARLY PRACTICE

Now our newcomer to the game knows how to play it, has acquired a racket, some tennis shoes that have not got black soles, and ball. Next he or she must go on to a court and start the serious business of hitting a ball with a racket against a wall, which is basically what squash is all about. It is, at all stages, good for a beginner's confidence if he attempts what he can probably achieve without too much difficulty, and at first it is much more use to go up very close to the front wall and have very simple rallies against it, hitting the ball a number of times successfully, than try to be too clever, start too far back in the court, and not be able to get any sort of rally going at all.

As the front of the court rallies improve, so the player can move gradually further back, with confidence and having built sound foundations. Remember to practise both forehand and backhand, and always hit forehand shots from the forehand side of the court and vice versa. Never make the mistake of running round a backhand. It may, initially, be weaker than the forehand, but this simply means that it needs more practice, which it fails to get if its owner keeps avoiding it!

Normally, a player who has played some other racket game, or even any game involving a ball, has very little difficulty in hitting a squash ball. Before doing anything more ambitious, it is useful to set oneself small targets; for instance, can one hit ten consecutive backhands, without either missing the ball, or pulling it across to the forehand side of the court. When this comes easily, move further back in the court, and closer to the side wall, and set a more difficult target of shots, which must return between the player and the wall. Once rallies and games start in earnest, beginners soon learn that the basic 'bread and butter' shots in squash are those, which hit the ball up and down the court, as close to the side wall as possible, so this early practice is useful for the future of one's own shots, and for returning the type of stroke that opponents will be playing.

So far I have dealt with the natural type of player or the one with previous ball game experience, neither of whom has any difficulty in hitting a squash ball, at least after a fashion. But what about the person with no great natural 'ball eye' and who has never played this type of game before? At first, such a player may well have the greatest difficulty in making contact with the ball at all, and fans fresh air every time the ball is dropped or thrown for him. After only a very short period of this, the wretched, cold, depressed victim may understandably pack it in and go fishing! This is a pity, because very often people who have begun like this have nevertheless turned into most competent, and even very successful players. But how can they get over this first hurdle?

The reason why a perfectly intelligent person cannot do something as basically simple as hit a ball with a racket, is usually because his eyes are not used to focusing on two moving objects some two feet away from where his arm normally ends! Nor may his brain have had previous experience of co-ordinating all the various nerves, muscles, tendons and so on, needed to swing a weapon through a given piece of air at a precise moment: 'precise', because it is only at that moment when a small round piece of rubber will be there. Add a bit of nervous tension, due to keenness to do well and fear of making a fool of oneself, and you have all the ingredients necessary for a complete miss!

How can we overcome this? As the difficulty experienced is simply a failure to make contact between racket head and ball, it can be overcome by ensuring this contact by getting the player to hold out his racket and placing the ball on the strings. He must then balance it there, stationary at first, and then while moving his arm. This is giving his eyes concentrated practice at seeing ball and racket in contact at various ranges, so that he will be able to judge better the sort of racket swing to allow, according to the distance the ball is from his body, when he comes to more orthodox practice. When he is able to retain the ball on the racket satisfactorily, he can then begin to bounce it gently up and down on the strings. At first, it need only be a couple of inches, on the old principle of starting with something easy, and then worked up as confidence and racket control develop. Soon it will be possible to move close to a wall, and instead of bouncing the ball up and down, bounce it on to the wall. Once the beginner can do this, he does get off the ground and can practise in the same way as the more proficient members of his group.

To begin with, it does not matter too much whether a beginner finds it easier to start with volleys against a wall, or more gentle shots, allowing the ball to bounce. Sometimes, the rather lower bounce of a squash ball can cause some difficulty at first, though this should be eased by the choice of the faster ball. But, however, the player does begin, he must include practice at both volleys and balls, which have bounced, as soon as he can, again remembering to do both on forehand and backhand.

As soon as a player can begin to hit the ball roughly where he wants to most of the time, he should start having rallies with someone else; after all, the aim is to get him to match play level as soon as possible, and the sooner he becomes used to someone else hitting the ball at him, the better. Then, as soon as possible, these practice rallies should turn into actual games, into which the beginners can introduce the various shots and tactics as they learn them.

3. The Service

In order to begin playing proper games of squash, a beginner has to learn how to serve. The rules governing the service are a little complicated, and before discussing the best ways of actually producing the shot, a player must be told what he may or may not do. You will remember that I said earlier that all the lines on the floor, plus the line across the middle of the front wall, are there simply for the service. The names of these lines are as follows: the line across the front wall is known as the 'cut' line, the one across the middle of the court, parallel with the front wall, is the 'short' line, and the one dividing the rear half of the court into two is the 'half court' line. On each side of the court, there are two service boxes marked out. These are two squares on the rear side of the short line, and are the areas from which Hand in must actually deliver the service.

The easiest way to remember the service rules is to keep in mind the number 3. There are three things which Hand in has to get right for a service to be good, three ways in which he may serve a single fault, and, unlike other games, three ways in which he can serve such a bad service that it is counted as a double fault and he loses the rally outright, with no second chance at all.

A GOOD SERVICE

Let us first of all discuss the things that have to be right for the service to be correct. Hand in must be standing in the appropriate service box, the ball must strike the right part of the front wall direct from the racket, and must rebound into the correct part of the court. To go into rather greater detail, Hand in is allowed to begin each 'hand' from whichever side he chooses, and will normally elect to serve into his opponent's backhand, to gain any marginal advantage that this may offer. While he remains in hand, he must alternate the sides for each new rally, so that if he begins serving from the right-hand service box and wins that rally, he must then serve from the left, and so on. The only exception to this rule is at the start of a new game. Then, although Hand in retains the service after winning the previous game, he does not have to serve from the side opposite to the one from which he ended the last game, but may restart from whichever side he chooses.

If, inadvertently, during a game he serves from the wrong side, and Hand out does not object, and the rally is played out, that rally stands, and if Hand in wins it, he must now alternate, as though he had served from the correct side. Normally, if there is a marker, he will prevent this from happening, and also Hand out will normally comment in time.

Assuming that Hand in has arrived at the appropriate box, he must now avoid the foot fault snags. The rule requires Hand in to have at least a part of one foot actually in contact with the floor, completely within the services box, at the moment when the ball is struck. He may, if he wishes, have both feet inside the box, but one is sufficient, and the other may be anywhere he likes. But the one that is inside must be grounded wholly within the box, and no part of it may be touching any of the lines, or the wall, or the floor outside. Thus, the tip of the toe in contact with the floor is enough to satisfy the rule, whereas the whole foot flat on the ground, with the heel touching a line, is a footfault. Part of the foot may be in the air over a line, as long as it is not touching it, and the bit that is touching the floor is completely within the line. Remember that most footfaults are committed by

31

players who look carefully at their foot position prior to serving, and check that all is well, and then, while actually in the act of hitting the ball, lift or drag their foot, so that at the actual moment of hitting it, they are infringing the rule, to their great surprise and indignation!

Then the ball has to be struck cleanly on to the front wall, in the upper panel between the out of court line and the cut line. Remember, again, that the lines are 'wrong' in squash, and that the ball, to be a good service, must not touch either of these lines.

The third requirement is that the ball shall rebound, so that it lands within the opposite back quarter of the court, from the serving box from which it was delivered; at this stage, it may hit either the side wall or the back wall, or both, provided its first contact with the floor is in the correct area. Remember that the quarter of the court means the area enclosed by the short line and the half court line, and it includes the service box, so that although it would be a fault if the ball landed on the short or half court lines, it is all right to touch the rear lines of the service box, which, of course, is not being used for this rally.

SINGLE FAULTS

So much for the correct service; now for the single fault, which, as in tennis, allows Hand in a second chance. The three types are a footfault, a ball which strikes the front wall on or below the cut line but above the tin, or a ball which does not land correctly within the opposite back quarter of the court. Any combination of two or all three of these errors is still only one single fault, so that to serve a double fault in this way Hand in has to serve two consecutive faults; he cannot lose the service by combining more than one single fault in the one shot. There are, however, two important points, which concern Hand out. Unlike tennis, he may, if he wishes, choose to volley the service, and if he does so, he automatically makes the service correct, even if it might have bounced eventually outside the correct area. Secondly, he has the option of accepting a single fault, and indeed he will frequently wish to do so, because it is likely to be a poor shot, which will give him a good chance of playing an aggressive return, whereas if he leaves it, and allows Hand in a second service, the latter will probably concentrate and put in a good, accurate shot, which could be troublesome.

If he does choose to take a fault, he merely plays a shot at the ball; he should not say anything, but once he has committed himself by playing at the ball, he cannot then claim any sympathy if he hits it down. If he accepts the service, he makes it 'correct', and if that rally should end in a let, Hand in starts again with a clean sheet. On the other hand, if he refuses to take a single fault, and the second service is good, and begins a rally which ends in a let, then Hand in does still have to remember that he has a single fault against his name, which will remain until that point has been finally decided, and however many lets there may be, another single fault will put him out. A let, of course, is a rally which has come to an end for some reason other than one of the players winning it. It could be because the ball has broken, one of the players has been distracted, or there has been a collision on court, but in any case the referee has decided that the fair thing to do is to replay it.

DOUBLE FAULTS

Now for the double faults, which lose Hand in the service in just the one stroke. First of all, it is a double fault if the ball does not at least clear the tin on the front wall. This covers anything from a complete miss, via a shot that drops on the floor to one that actually hits the tin or its board. Secondly, it is a double fault if the ball hits a side wall on its way to the front wall, and thirdly if the ball goes out of court, i.e. hits anything on or above the out of court lines.

LOB SERVICE

We have now covered the rules that deal with the service, and must go on to discuss how best to play the shot. There are basically two types of service at squash, which for ease of definition, I will call the lob service and the defensive service. Unlike tennis, there is no such thing as an 'ace' service, which the receiver simply cannot return. With a wall to bounce the ball against, it is just not possible to blast the ball past one's opponent. All one can do at squash is to make the service as difficult as possible. It cannot be a winner unless Hand out co-operates and makes a mistake, so one must try and give him the maximum chance of doing just that! The most difficult shots to play in squash are those which are played close to a wall. This is for two reasons; not only is one inhibited in swinging the racket, and if one does hit the wall with it, a complete mishit may result, but also the ball itself is less easy to judge, and one's range of shots is severely limited.

Thus one's aim with the service is to keep the ball close to the walls, place it as far into the back corner of the court as possible, and leave Hand out to worry. The best service, if the height of the roof of the court allows, is the high lob service. This can be made to drop very steeply, and forces the opponent to take it well towards the back wall for the simple reason that it is too high for him to reach any further forward. It should also be made to hit the side wall, so that it is not only descending rapidly, but coming off at an angle. Then it should bounce in front of the back wall, and this, plus the striking on the side wall, should take speed off the ball, so that if it is allowed to hit the back wall it will not rebound far enough for Hand out to get it up. He is, therefore, forced to play 'across the line' of the ball in a very restricted space, and you have done what you set out to do, which was to give him the maximum chance of making a mistake!

'Hitting across the line' is a cricket expression, which applies to all ball games. If one's weapon, be it a bat or a racket, is moved along the straight line on which the ball is approaching, the two are bound to meet sooner or later. If it moves across this line of approach, it will only hit the ball if it happens to cross the line at the precise moment when the ball is there. It follows that, if you can force an opponent to hit across the line, he will be more likely to miss the ball. The line of approach of the good lob service is downwards and across the court; hitting back up this line would send the ball straight into the roof! The probable aim of the returner of the service is to play a straight shot parallel to the side wall, and this is in itself a risk against the accurate lob.

DEFENSIVE SERVICE

However, sometimes the roof of the court is too low, or the lights dangle down further than most, or the ball is so fast and volatile that there is a great risk of it soaring out of court, and in such conditions the advantages of the lob service are more than outweighed by the risks attached to attempting it. When this happens, the defensive service is the answer.

Here, the aims are very different. To be safe, Hand in hits the ball only just comfortably above the cut line, and aims to bring it back on a path fairly close to the opposite side wall, to as 'good a length' as possible. I should explain that a 'good length' in squash refers to a stroke, which causes the opponent to be caught in two minds over whether to try and take the ball before it reaches the back wall, or to leave it, and not be sure, whether it will rebound far enough for him to get it back if he does so. So, once again, the aim is to put the ball close to a wall and to embarrass Hand out in the back corner of the court. This is less of a problem than a good lob service can set, but played accurately, this kind of service can ensure a defensive and not very ambitious return, and can give Hand in the initiative in the rally.

METHOD OF PLAYING

The actual method of playing the strokes varies considerably.

35

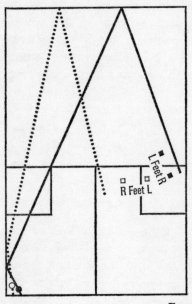

———— *Foot position and flight of lob service.*
······· *Foot position and flight of defensive service.*
● ○ *Bounce position*

FIG. 2.

For the lob service, one should stand as far forward and as near the side wall as is comfortable, and the ball should be struck forehand on one's forehand side and backhand on the other side. The reason for this is that one wants to widen the angle on the front wall. This will ensure a more direct blow on the side wall, thus taking more speed off the ball, and also ensure a wide angle on the back wall, so that, if the ball is allowed to get there, it will slide along the wall, and not rebound far enough to be retrieved. Hand in should stand still to serve; too many people stroll into the service box, serving as they go, merely as a way of getting the next rally started! Just as it is easier to hit a target, if one lies down and takes aim, so it is easier to put a squash ball where one wants to, if one steadies oneself, thinks about it and plays the shot in a balanced and deliberate way. The server should be standing rather more 'open' than in the stance I described earlier for hitting the ball down the wall, because he is now

36

aiming to hit it across court. In fact, he can stand almost facing the front corner of the court nearest to him. The ball should be hit underarm, and not as a tennis service, and it is more of an upward action than a hard hit.

The ball should hit the front wall about half-way across and about half-way between the cut line and the out of court line, that is to say, somewhere near the centre spot of the top 'panel' on the front wall. It should still be rising then, and should continue to do so as it comes back down the court, and this is where the height of the roof is vital. It should hit the side wall as close to the out of court line as can be safely judged, to bounce in front of the back wall. The apparent vagueness with all the 'abouts' and 'somewhere near' over where to hit the front wall is not simply uncertainty on my part; there is no one magic spot, which is always the ideal point to aim at, because the conditions vary so much. Which is *exactly* the best spot depends on the speed of the ball, the height of the roof, the conditions of the walls, and even the physical size of the person serving, but this gives a starting place for working out the ideal on any given day, with any given ball, on any court.

The aims and intentions of the defensive service are quite different, and so the shot itself is quite different. Whereas the aim with the lob service was to widen the angle on the front wall, the aim now is to narrow it. Consequently, instead of serving as far forward and as near to the side wall as possible, one should now serve from further back, and the ball should be struck as near the centre of the court as comfortable. To do this, it is necessary to hit the ball as a backhand shot from the forehand side of the court, and vice versa. The ball should now be aimed at a spot about (here we go again!) three-quarters of the way across the front wall, and a couple of feet above the cut line, hard enough for that particular ball to carry to a good length at the back of the court, and hit the side wall approximately half-way between the short line and the back wall. This means that the opponent will need to take the ball very close to the side wall, which at least will limit his range of shots, and may well induce a mishit.

At first, the beginner may not find it easy to serve on the backhand, especially when trying to produce a lob service from that side of the court. So, just to begin with, it is all right to serve forehand strokes from both sides of the court, but only until the backhand gains in confidence, when it should be used as regularly as the forehand, depending on what is required at that moment.

OTHER POINTS ABOUT THE SERVICE

There are, of course, other types of service, but none is as good as the two types described so far. Their only value is as a surprise weapon, to break up the concentration of a player, who seems to have a good answer to your more orthodox services. Thus, the occasional hard hit service, or the one down the centre of the court, or even the high, hard hit service, played from wide out towards the front of the court and hit so that it hits the front wall, then the side wall on the server's own side of the court, where it careers across at an unusual angle, can all have a value as surprise shots. If overdone, and so anticipated, they can give Hand out the advantage, and although it is useful to be able to vary the service occasionally, the accent is very definitely on the 'occasionally', and these varieties must not be overdone.

Regrettably, in good class squash, it often happens that the players do not bother much about their services and simply get the ball into play any old how. The reason is that matches are usually played on hot courts, or the ball has warmed up so that it is bouncing a lot. In these circumstances, the lob service is a risk and the defensive service does not create many problems for your opponent. Nevertheless, I do believe that, over a whole match, the player who thinks and bothers about his service every time will show a profit over the one who does not do so. Every now and again, he will gain the initiative in a rally and win it, and these could be the vital rallies on which a close match depends. And, of course, when he gets back on a cooler court, his good service will really pay dividends. So do bother about it; it is the first shot of every rally, and as such sets the tone of the rally and gives one player or the other the initiative!

4. The Return

If the service is the most important shot of the rally, because it is the first, and should give Hand in the initiative, then the second most important is the return of service. This is Hand out's first shot, and he has either to defend well against a good service by playing a safe return, which denies Hand in the advantage he was hoping for, or he has to attack a bad service, and either attempt to play a winner or at least grasp the initiative for himself.

Obviously, until Hand in has actually served, Hand out will not know whether it is going to be a good or a bad service, or indeed, a lob or a hard hit or any other variety. So he has to start off by assuming the worst, and by being prepared to play a safe shot to a perfect service. If it turns out to be anything less than that, he can adapt to a more attacking stroke, but the first priority must be to get the ball back and the rally going. Consequently, I am going to concentrate in this chapter on the particular point of dealing with a good service. A bad service is no problem, and can be attacked by whichever one of the normal strokes we shall discuss later seems most appropriate to its speed and direction, and to the position of the opponent.

POSITIONING

We have already agreed that, unlike tennis, there is no such thing in squash as an 'ace' service. The only time a service is a winner is when Hand out co-operates by making a misjudgement. Hand in is, therefore, doing his best to make it as easy as possible for Hand out to make such a mistake, and Hand out must make it as easy for himself as he can not to do so. His initial position is the first thing to consider. Naturally, if he were to stand in the corner of the court, perhaps thinking he was defending the most vulnerable area, Hand in would hit the ball hard, straight at him, and he would be left with no room to swing his racket, and would only be able to jab feebly at the ball as it approached his midriff. Also, if he were to go too far up the court, with the apparently laudable idea of taking the ball early on the volley, Hand in should be able to lob it over his head, and he will then be forced to run backwards, looking up at the ball as it drops out of the lights, and wondering when he himself is going to crash into the back wall. So I always suggest to beginners that they will make things much easier for themselves, if they stand just inside the centre rear corner of the quarter of the court into which Hand in is serving. If they stand close to the back wall, it is much easier to anticipate whereabouts the ball will hit the back wall, if allowed to do so.

This does not take very long to learn, and just standing near the back wall and hitting a few high shots back to yourself can give you good practice in judging a service. What one must avoid is allowing a service to drop into the 'nick' between the back wall and the floor, or to bounce on the floor and then go on to the back wall, because it may then not have enough speed to rebound far enough from the wall for it to be retrievable. So, from the length point of view, a good rule is never to allow the ball to go to the back wall, unless it is going to hit it at, or above, the height of one's own knees. This allows for a certain margin or error, and even if it does hit the back wall a little low, it will still be well above the nick and will rebound a convient distance. So allow the ball to go through to the back wall if it is going to hit it knee-high or above, but move forward and take it as it approaches the back wall if it is not going to do so.

I said just now that it was not easy to have to move backwards, and this is another reason why it is good sense to stand at a corner of the area, ready to move forward into it. You know that Hand in has to serve into that particular quarter of the court, so be in a position to move towards it. If you stand anywhere else, it is about even money whether you have to go forwards or backwards, so position yourself so you can guarantee being able to move forward.

The next thing I want you to try to imagine is a triangle. It starts from your position by the half court line, just inside the appropriate quarter of the court, and one line runs along parallel with the back wall and about a foot and a half from it. When it gets to the corner of the court it goes up parallel with the side wall, and at the same distance from it, stopping just short of the service box, and then a diagonal line forms the third side, coming back to your original position. This triangle is a three-dimensional affair and extends upwards as high as a player can reach. It represents a safe area within which Hand out can play a free stroke, uninhibited by the nearness of a wall, and it is an area through which the most perfect of services must pass at some stage. Nobody has yet patented a service which will run along the opposite side wall, and then turn at right angles and run along the back wall! So either the service will hit the side wall in front of the triangle and rebound into it, or it will pass through the front of the triangle on its way to an impossible position at the back of the court. In either case, Hand out should have been able to play it while it was in the triangle area.

Thus the essentials of returning even the best of services are: stand in the correct place, watch Hand in as he serves to give yourself advance notice of what type of service it will be, and to have the maximum time to judge its flight towards the back wall, and move forward into your triangle, in order to be in the right position to get that particular service at its most vulnerable moment. Of course, as you get more experienced, you will find that you are taking up your initial

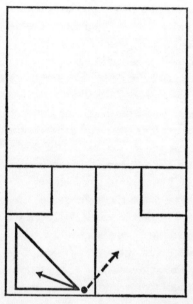

*Triangle represents area in
which it is safe to take a good
service. Note— →eyes watching
server, and ——→path forward
into triangle.*

FIG. 3.

position some way inside the triangle, but until your judge-
ment is good enough, I would advise you to play it safe. And
incidentally, remember that every time you miss a service
return because your racket has hit the wall, it is because you
tried to play the ball outside the triangle, instead of either
taking it before it got there, or waiting until it came for
enough off the wall for safety.

POSSIBLE RETURN STROKES

So far we have talked only about how to get into position to
play a stroke at a service, however good that service may be,
but now we must assume that the player has done everything
right so far, and is now waiting to be told what he must try
to do with the ball. Basically, the safest shot and usually the
best, is to hit the ball to as good a length as possible down
the side wall on that side of the court. The height of the
service, and its length, will decide whether you do this as a

high volley, a low volley or a normal drive, played after the ball has bounced. Hand out's aim now is to do exactly what Hand in has just tried to do to him, and which both will continue to do for most of the rally, and that is to 'embarrass' the opponent in the back corners of the court. Not only does the service have something to do with how he should attempt this, but also the speed of the ball and the height of the roof. The slower the ball, the higher it will have to be hit on the front wall, to ensure that it carries to the back; the faster the ball, the lower it should be hit, to prevent it rebounding a long way from the back wall, if allowed to get there.

However, even more important than the length of this return is the nearness of the ball to the side wall. Whereas we have just agreed that it is impossible for a server to hit a ball from the other side of the court and miss the triangle, it is now perfectly possible, from the same side of the court as the triangle itself, to keep the ball so close to the wall that it does run along inside it, thus forcing the opponent to play his shot from the danger area in which there is a good chance of striking the wall with the racket, and the consequent risk of a mishit.

One thing must be remembered on return of service. If the ball has bounced, the perfectly normal backhand drive is used, the basic backhand learnt the first lesson on court; but more often than not it will be necessary to volley the service, and this can be a dangerous shot for a beginner. You have to be careful to keep a firm, 'locked' wrist; a squash ball and racket do not behave as the tennis ball and racket do, and a squash volley, whether you are trying a hard hit or a soft shot, has to be played firmly. For the expert, there are varieties, brought about by 'slicing' across the ball in flight, but that comes much later, and in any case, even in these shots, the racket head is kept high. It is not always easy to do this, especially on the high volley, but if you analyse the services you see people hitting down on the volley, you will realise that, everytime, the racket head has been pulled right

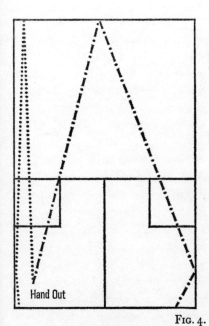

*The safest returns of service -
down the side wall to a good
length, or high across court
into the opposite back corner.*

Hand Out

FIG. 4.

down. It can simply be a bad follow-through which finishes up by the ankles somewhere as the ball hits the tin, or more often is caused by a 'flyswat' stroke, in which the wrist is loose. If the ball is hit late, it goes in the roof; if early, into the floor; and only if the contact between racket and ball happens to be a just the right moment will the ball go where intended. Of course the racket can be angled to hit the ball across court, if required, but at the end of a high volley, the racket should be pointing towards the top of the front wall, where it joins the nearest side wall.

There are other perfectly good returns of service, though the one down the side wall is the safest and the most usual. It is often a good idea to hit the ball high into the opposite back corner of the court, as a sort of service in reverse. Once again, the aim is to cause problems for the opponent in the back corner, and the shot is played in a very similar way to the service itself. However, whereas the service is being hit

45

with Hand out probably standing fairly far back in the court, Hand out is now returning the compliment with Hand in standing in the centre of the court, as you will shortly learn he should do. Thus, a low service will still get to the back of the court and is not a particularly vulnerable shot, but the low return of service, across court, is dangerous, because Hand in will be in position to chop it off for a winner in the front of the court.

Consequently, although the lob return of a service is a very useful shot, it simply must be played high, and well over the possible reach of an opponent in the centre of the court; it is a high, rather than a hard hit, shot. Neither now, nor at any time in the rally, will you be able to blast a ball past the other player in the centre of the court. Like the impossibility of reproducing the tennis service ace, so too is the hard cross court shot more likely to be a loser than a winner. The front wall takes off so much pace, the opponent has longer to see it on the way, and even if it does pass him, there is still a good chance of getting it back as it rebounds from the back wall.

I said earlier that it is possible to play an attacking shot off the service in order to try to play a winner, or to wrest the initiative from Hand in. The most usual are the attempts to play the ball short into one of the front corners, again either on the volley, or as a 'drop shot', which we will discuss in the next chapter. Any shot is possible for the poor length service, and one's choice is determined by what your own best shot is from that position, and where your opponent is weakest. But do always remember that you are Hand out, and anything too ambitious, involving too big a risk, can lead to the ball going down, and your opponent scoring a point.

One shot, I think, must be explained in detail, before we leave the return of service, and that is the boast shot out of the back corners of the court. Sometimes you will misjudge a service, or during the rally the opponent will play a good lob or passing shot into the back corner, and you will just have

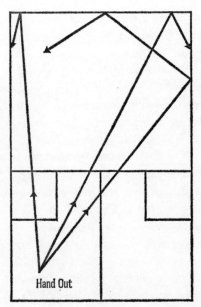

The aggressive returns of service; the short volleys and the reverse angle. The same shots can be played, even if the ball has bounced, as ground strokes.

Hand Out

FIG. 5.

to get it out. The difficulty, of course, lies in the nearness of the back wall, which prevents you from taking a full swing of your racket, which you need to 'lever' the ball thirty feet to the front wall again.

The technique, here, is to play a more or less normal drive at the ball, but of course you have to reposition your body, so that your normal racket swing does not hit the back wall. This means hitting the ball towards the side wall, but as you want to get it towards the front, and all you have done so far is put yourself in a position to play a powerful shot, you have to do one or both of two things. Go back first of all to your early days of practising the basic forehand and backhand. You will remember that sometimes you pulled the ball across court unintentionally. This was either because you hit it in front of your leading foot, or your wrist brought the head of the racket round too far. Now, in the corner of the court, this is precisely what you need to do deliberately!

47

So, as you play your drive, apparently into the side wall, you help it round towards the front by hitting it in front of the leading foot, which is taking it early, and, if possible, you help it even further forward with a wrist flick at the moment of making contact with the ball.

In fact, when I am coaching, I usually get my beginners to face even further round than necessary to play the normal drive into the side wall. I tell them to actually face the opposite side wall, so that the ball is almost behind their backs. Then I make them bend low on the leg nearest to the back wall, and hit the ball hard, upwards and as far forward on the side wall as possible, letting the racket head overtake the wrist to provide the flick forward. This may sound as though I am making life unnecessarily difficult for them, but there are two great advantages to getting used to playing the ball from this position. One is that, during a rally, a player may be running very hard in an attempt to get the ball up; he may have time to lunge towards the back wall on his front foot, but not have time to get his whole body parallel to the back wall, and this applies, too, if he is passed, and has to flick the ball up from behind him, when he has not got time to get back for it, and it will not come off the back wall. Secondly, when a ball is bouncing about in a corner of the court, it is only too easy to misjudge its bounce off a wall, or guess wrong which wall it will hit first. If you get into the original position, with your feet and body parallel to the back wall, and the ball leaps out further from the side wall than you expected, then it will come into your body too far for you to play much of a shot. In my position, the one foot can be moved further towards the centre of the court, to give room behind the body, and the same shot played.

The two most common mistakes made in the back corners are, firstly, running into the corner itself and not giving yourself room to get the leverage of your arm and racket necessary to hoist the ball to the front, and secondly, trying to hit the ball too hard. Blasting the thing into the side wall is no help at all, and all that will happen is that you will see the ball gently trickling across the court somewhere near the middle of the court. In squash, remember it is not hitting the ball hard against a wall that causes it to rebound a long way from it; it is hitting it upwards against that wall, so that it carries on in the air. So in the boast shots, hit the ball upwards on to the side wall, so that it will gain height and have a chance of carrying to the front wall.

5. Elementary Tactics in a Rally

Now that we have discussed the service and return of service in some detail, we can assume that the rally is well and truly launched, and we must now discuss what happens during the rally. Tactics now come into it. After all, the service is struck from a definite position in the court, as required by the rules, and as it has to go into a certain area, the return of service is also a more or less static shot. From then on either player may hit the ball wherever and however he wishes, and may run all over the court. So we now have to decide how best to advise a player to move around the court in order to cover as many of his opponent's shots as possible, and how best to get into position to play his own winning strokes, and also what shots he should have in his repertoire in order to place the ball where his opponent least wants it.

I divide 'Tactics' in squash into two distinct categories: the first, which I want to discuss in this chapter, are elementary tactics, and refer to things which are always sound and correct in any game of squash. The second are match tactics, which vary in every game depending on the variables such as the court on which the match is being played, the speed of the ball, the strength and weaknesses of one's opponent, one's own fitness and so on. These we will come to later.

'OAK TREE' AND 'BLINKERS'
There are two very vital elementary tactics, in addition to having a good service and safe return of service, and being fast and fit physically, and I have always nicknamed them

'Oak tree' and 'Blinkers'. The 'oak tree' is an attempt to sum up the whole question of correct positioning in the court, and 'blinkers' is my way of trying to get over to people the importance of watching the ball.

The oak tree first. Try to imagine a large oak tree, planted right in the centre of the court, with its circumference going round just inside the service boxes, and with the top sawn off at about twelve feet. It represents the area which can be reached by the average player when standing with one foot on the 'T' formed by the lines joining in the centre of the court. If you now realise that, if one player is in this central position, his opponent cannot be there too, you will see that a player allowed to play a stroke from the oak tree has a very good chance of making a winner. As his opponent is not on the 'T', he must be in one of the four quarters of the court, and whichever one he is in, a shot to the diametrically opposite corner will either be a winner, or at least make him cover a great deal of ground.

A number of facts emerge from this; firstly, it is essential to prevent one's own shots from returning from the front wall into the oak tree area, because such a shot will present the opponent with a likely winner. So the ball must be hit down the side walls past the oak tree, high over the top, or close to the front wall and short of it. Secondly, it is vital after every shot, from the service onwards, to race back to the 'T' in order to plant one's own oak tree; not only does one want to be there in order to play a winner, if the other person gives the chance by bringing the ball back to the oak tree, but it is also, from a defensive point of view, the most central position from which to reach any corner of the court to which the opponent may have hit the ball. Thirdly, and this is perhaps rather an advanced point for this stage, it is a good idea to hit shots, which pull the opponent away from the 'T' in such a way as to give one a clear run to it. Sometimes a player will play a shot, which is well away from the danger area, but which enables, or even forces, his opponent to play

51

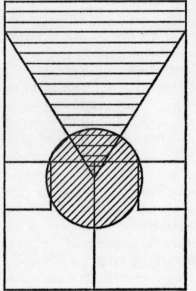

////// Oaktree
▭▭▭ Arc of vision of player
on 'T' with blinkers on.

FIG. 6.

the ball from a position which cuts off the player from the centre of the court.

Now for 'blinkers'. Everyone knows the saying 'Watch the ball', but games like tennis, badminton, table tennis and cricket have made us used to the idea of watching the ball, which is coming towards us. In squash, however, the majority of an opponent's shots are hit from the back of the court, or should be if one is playing well, and the player himself is on the 'T'. So it is even more vitally important in squash to stress the idea of watching the ball. You have only to walk along the gallery of any club in the country, and watch quite useful players, to see how many of them are 'front wall gazers', even when the opponent and the ball are behind them. These people are like horses with blinkers on; they are limiting their own vision and halving their anticipation by not watching the ball all the time. If you stare at the centre of the front wall, you can see the whole of it, plus a few feet

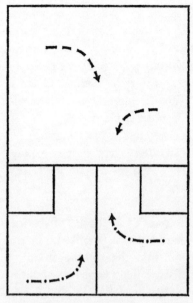

Correct movements to 'T' if ball has been hit so that it will return into the same quarter of the court.

FIG. 7.

of the side wall. As you have no idea what sort of shot the other player has attempted, you cannot tell which part of the front wall the ball will hit, or how hard, so even when the ball does arrive in your arc of vision, it will take a valuable second to focus and register exactly what it is doing, and get the body moving towards it.

A player with blinkers on is vulnerable to any shot, but in particular to the drop shot from the back of the court or the hard hit down the wall. The first no sooner appears than it hits the front wall, and drops dead, long before he can register and take action, and the second darts in and out of the player's view before he can possibly 'fix' it, and tell what it is doing. Now, take the blinkers off, and make him watch the ball right on to his opponent's racket. He will now see whether the opponent is playing a gentle drop shot, and will instinctively be moving up towards the front wall in readiness, or will see the full swing of a hard hit, and again be moving

53

automatically in the right direction. He will also be able to see if his shot into the back of the court has done anything unexpected; for example, it may have bounced out from the side wall further than he anticipated, and he will now be able to move away from the centre of the court and avoid being hit by his opponent. With his blinkers on, he would never know the danger he was in until too late.

To sum up these two points then, remember always to get to the 'T' as quickly as you can after every shot you play, and when you have got there, do watch the ball all the time.

DROP STROKES

Once again, as I did when talking about the return of service, I have begun by explaining where a player should be in the court, and how he can best get into the right position to play the ball. Now we must discuss the various possibilities open to him once he has arrived at the right spot and found the ball conveniently placed to hit. What are the various strokes? Very simply, there are four types of shot, but as these can be played towards either side of the court, this means eight shots; at least, there are eight possible strokes when the player is in a position clear of the walls. When he is very close to a wall, his choice is limited probably to one or two. However, let us take a position, for example somewhere in the front quarter of the court, well clear of the wall.

The first pair of shots are the drops. A drop shot is one aimed to hit the front wall very low, just above the tin, and very softly, so that it will not rebound very far. Usually it is aimed towards the side wall closest to the player, with the aim of the ball rebounding from the front wall into the nick between the side wall and the floor. Obviously it will stay even closer to the front wall, and be therefore more difficult for the opponent to reach, if it can hit both the floor and the side wall to take way off. Remember, too, that a ball will bounce further from any wall, side or back, if it hits the wall before the floor, and will stay closer to that wall if it hits the floor first. So the aim is not only to pull your opponent as far up the court as possible, but also to pull him right over to the side wall. This may add to his problems, as he has the maximum distance to run, and also is more likely to mishit a ball, which is low and close to a wall, than one which may be low, but at least is out in the open. So, aim for the nick, but err on the side of making the ball bounce on the floor before it hits the side wall. As far as the execution of the shot is concerned, it is played in a similar way on the backhand and forehand. The ball must be stroked, and not pushed or jabbed at, just as in the basic forehand and backhand strokes learned on the first day. The ball should be hit about level with the front foot with a horizontal racket, and guided towards the corner.

You will notice that I said that the shot should be played with the racket horizontal; there are three points about this. In the first place, if you get used to playing shots with a vertical racket, it means that you yourself have to get much closer to the ball, and therefore have to move further each time, instead of making use of the full reach of your arm and racket. Over the period of a long match you would have had to cover a great deal more ground than you need have done, and when stamina is beginning to tell in the latter stages, this could count against you. Secondly, and just as important, you can get to the ball that fraction of a second sooner, if you are reaching for it with arm and racket, then if you have to wait until you have taken the extra step necessary to get close to the ball, and this may make all the difference between giving the other player just time to get to your shot, and playing a winner. Thirdly, and perhaps most important of all, it is not easy to hit winners in the limited space of a squash court, and one of the most effective ways of doing so is to wrongfoot the opponent. This can best be done by last minute changes of direction, when he has been led to suppose that the ball is going to one side, and you play

55

it to the other. Such deceptions depend almost entirely on use of the wrist, and only if your wrist is in position to manoeuvre the racket, so that the ball may be hit early or late, softly or hard, can these be achieved. The optimum position, where the wrist has most flexibility, is when the racket is horizontal.

My reason for sidetracking like this is to try and make clear why it is important to play all the shots basically the same way. It is easy for you to make last-minute alterations if you hear your opponent moving in a certain direction, and it is difficult for him to anticipate where you are going to hit the ball. So, to return to the drop shot, do play it as a proper stroke, with a back swing and follow through like any other, so that you can turn it into some other shot, if you suddenly wish to, and so that your opponent cannot guess that it is a drop shot coming. Some people take speed off the ball by opening the face of the racket, which means turning it so that the leading face is pointing upwards, and this tends to cut the racket under the ball. This not only reduces the effect of the racket on the ball, but also imparts cut to the ball, which, as a result, will tend to bounce downwards off the front wall, and thus remain closer to it. Other people play the shot with a locked wrist, so that the arm and racket are rigid and impart no pace to the ball. As with all shots, practice on your own, bearing in mind the end product that you are aiming at from any particular shot, will show you how you find it best and easiest to produce that shot. The basics, however, are to play a smooth stroke, to bend the front leg in order to get the racket more or less horizontal at the height of the ball when you are going to hit it, to transfer the weight forward as you play the stroke, and to follow through upwards, and not 'round the corner', across court.

I said that usually the drop is played towards the side wall nearest to the player, and there are two main reasons for this. One is that it is a delicate shot requiring considerable

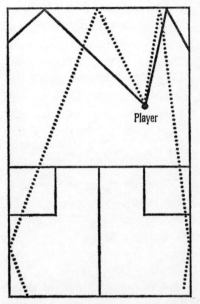

Four of the Eight Possible Shots:

———— *the straight and cross court drops.*

·········· *the cross court lob, and the 'loop' shot down the wall.*

Player

FIG. 8.

accuracy, and it is easier to achieve this over a short distance than a longer one, and so easier to play a good drop to the nearer side than the further one. The other is that the opponent may anticipate it correctly and arrive in time to hit the ball, while you are still not very far from where you played it. Obviously it will be more difficult for him to play a winner past you in the narrow space between you and the closer side wall than if you open it up for him by playing it to the further side wall, and give him half the court in which to attempt a winner. Nevertheless, a cross court drop can be a very useful surprise shot, especially if you know your opponent is out of position for it. The two drop shots are very valuable weapons, and no player is complete until he can play them from most positions in the court, forehand or backhand.

Remember, too, that it is easier to play a genuine drop shot when the ball has bounced, and you are able to hit it at the

57

top of its bounce, and that it is a dangerous shot to play as a volley. It is really only worth trying when you know for a fact that it is a certain winner, and you have not the time to let it bounce. One of the basic truths of squash is the obvious one, that the court is longer than it is wide, and so an opponent is going to get more tired if he is made to run up and down it, than simply across from side to side. The drop shot is one of the main ways of pulling him up to the front of the court. It must, however, be played well, because a bad drop, bouncing about in the open spaces, merely presents the opponent with a wide range of easy winners. It is not, therefore, worth playing unless you yourself are balanced and able to play it accurately and well. If in doubt, or at full stretch, do not attempt a 'touch' stroke.

ANGLE STROKES

The second pair of strokes I want to discuss are the angles. A defensive angle shot from the back of the court is often known as a 'boost' or 'boast', because the ball is boosted upwards off the side wall towards the front, but elsewhere in the court an ordinary, or 'straight' angle shot is one which is hit at the side wall nearest to the player, and a 'reverse' angle is one which is pulled across court on to the side wall furthest from the player. Any sort of angle shot, therefore, is one which hits a side wall first, and thus approaches the front wall at an angle, rather than direct from the racket. The main offensive use of angle shots is to wrongfoot the opponent. If, for example, you are in front of him, and have been hitting the ball hard down the wall to the back of the court, and shape up for the current stroke in exactly the same way, he is likely to assume that this too will go down the wall, and he will have begun to move in anticipation. If you can then either hit the ball late, or angle your racket by using your wrist, and strike it into the side wall, it will then go across court to the diametrically opposite corner from the one to which he is running. Again, if you have been playing

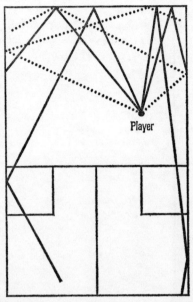

The Other Four
———— the hard hit shots
(drive or short kill)
········ the angle and reverse
angle.

Player

FIG. 9.

drop shots towards the side wall nearest to you from positions in the front of the court, he is likely to begin to anticipate these, and to move up between you and the side wall, in the hope of getting to the ball so quickly he can play a winner, before you can recover. If you hear him coming, or guess that he may do so, you can play the ball on to the side wall, so that it goes across in front of you, and bounces twice on the other side of the court from the one to which he has moved.

The angle shots are the best and easiest way to wrongfoot an opponent, but as such, they must be used in contrast to other shots, and not overdone. This applies particularly to the reverse angles. Because you are hitting completely across the line of the ball in order to pull it to the other side of the court, there must be an element of risk attached to it, and the risk is only worth while if the likelihood of playing a winner, is high. So, have the reverse angles in your repertoire,

59

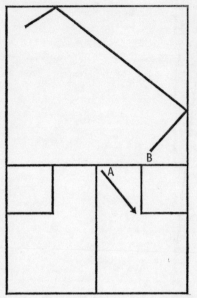

Use of Angles. A, on 'T,' anticipating hard shot down wall; B changes tactics and wrong foots him with an angle.

FIG. 10.

but do not overdo them. Use the others more frequently, but again, well mixed with straight drives, drops and other shots. The angle from the front of the court can be played in two ways; if it is the contrast to the drop shot, then fool your opponent as long as you can by preparing to play a soft shot very deliberately, and as he comes up for the drop, you flick the ball round to the other side of yourself. Similarly, if he is expecting a hard shot, go through all your usual preparations for a big hit, and in fact do hit the ball hard – but into the side wall, which will send it right across court, to die by the opposite wall.

In order to play an angle shot, your racket must be made to face the part of the side wall you intend to hit with the ball; it is absolutely essential that your basic foot and body positions remain as usual, or you will signal your intentions to your opponent, and this change in the direction of the shot must be achieved by the wrist. Once again, I suggest that you

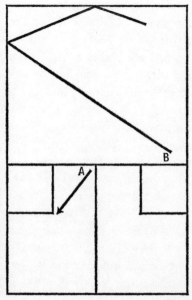

Use of Angles. A, on 'T,' anticipates hard cross court drive and is wrong footed by reverse angle.

go on court and find out your own best way of playing them, bearing in mind, where you want the ball to go, and that you must not do anything different in your moving to the ball, or in your early preparation for the shot. Some people need to play angles simply by playing the ball late, in other words when it has passed the front foot, and so cannot be hit straight to the front wall by the usual stroke; others, with stronger wrists, can achieve an angle by using the wrist and taking the ball earlier. This is preferable, as it may deny the opponent a fraction of a second's anticipation and movement time, and it also makes it more likely that the actual shot will be cloaked by the position of the player's body from his opponent in position on the 'T'.

One very valuable use of angles, is as a frequent shot on hot courts. We agreed, when talking about drop shots, that it is necessary to move an opponent up and down the court. One a hot court, when the ball is bouncing high and rebounding a long way from the walls, a drop shot is not only not so effective, it is highly dangerous. It is more difficult to play under these conditions, and is far less likely to produce a winner. More difficult, because a lively ball is much harder to control, as it is travelling faster when you hit it, and bouncing higher, both of which make a touch shot just above the tin a hazardous stroke; and less likely to be a winner, because, even if played very accurately, it will leap back from the front wall, and the opponent will probably get to it easily. We also agreed that a poor drop shot is simply a present to the other player, so on hot courts, drop shots are all risks and no profit. But there is still the need to move an opponent up and down the court, and this can be done by using angles. They need not be played so dangerously near the tin as drop shots and, because they are sliding across the face of the front wall, they will rebound less far from it then even the best of drops, and so become the ideal way of moving your opponent about when the ball is fast.

THE LOB

We now come to what I consider to be the most under-used shot in the game, the lob. It is basically the shot for getting you out of trouble. For instance, if your opponent has played a good shot, which you can only just reach at the front of the court, any shot other than a lob is asking for trouble, because your opponent is waiting behind you to hit his next stroke past you for a winner, and you cannot anticipate just where he is. A lob, however, gives you time to get back to the 'T' and start the rally again, so to speak. He cannot get at it to rush you until it has come down within his reach!

The lob is also the basic shot to fall back on, when you are temporarily out of breath or beginning to get tired. An opponent will find it difficult to speed up and chase around a player who is persistently slowing down the game by a campaign of lobbing, and in trying to do so he may well snatch at the ball and begin to mishit it.

So much for the defensive aspects of the lob; but it is not simply a last resort shot for when you are too tired or out of position to think of anything else. It can also be a most attacking stroke, with probably more chances of being a winner than any other shot, and when it is not a winner itself, it has a habit of producing a defensive return, which sets up a winner. The trouble is that it is dependent on the height of the roof of the court on which the match is being played. As too many courts still have low lights, beams or rafters, no player can depend solely on a style of play based on lobbing, or he will be lost on such courts. All the same, it is possible to lob on most courts, and every player should be able to play the shot well.

The stroke itself is played exactly as I described in the chapter on the service; it is not a hard-hit shot, but one hit upwards on to the front wall, with enough speed to carry it on from there over the oak tree to the opposite back corner of the court. Again, it is best if it can be made to hit the side wall, and then bounce on the floor before hitting the back wall, as this will ensure that it will not come off the wall far enough for the opponent to retrieve it, with any luck. In a rally, a good lob is an even more dangerous shot than a good service, because the opponent is in the centre of the court, instead of standing waiting for it. He now has to turn and run back, torn between watching the ball, and taking his eyes off it to see where the back wall is. No longer is he able to move forward, as the receiver of the service can do; now he must move backwards. All this adds to the likelihood of an error in judgment or a mishit, and the lob itself has longer to drop in an impossible position in the corner, because the opponent may not now have time to volley it while it is in the triangle we imagined for taking service. Also, if the lob is played from further up the court than the service box it can be made to come down more steeply than a service, and if the roof is high enough a lob can be virtually unplayable.

The idea, then, is to hit the ball high, over the oak tree and on to the opposite side wall near the back corner, where it drops as near dead as possible. Again, the exact spot on the front wall depends on where you are hitting it from, how fast the ball is, how high or low the roof is, and so on.

The second shot of the lob pair is much more of a defensive shot. It is the lob down the side wall nearest to the player. Because of this, the side wall cannot have the slowing-up effect of the opposite wall, because the ball will slide along it, and not really strike it. As it can never be such an effective shot, it is only played when the height of the roof makes the high cross court lob too dangerous. After all, if you are forced to avoid dangling lights, you have very little margin of error between hitting the light and hitting the top of the oak tree. So when a lob is the right shot under these circumstances, the only safe way to play it is down the wall, and not so high. Now, of course, it no longer has to go over the oak tree, so it does not need to be so lofted, and the aim must be to keep the ball as close to the side wall as possible, and play it to as good a length as possible in the back of the court. It is not as likely to be a winner as its brother, although every now and then one will cling to the side wall, or drop in the nick on the back wall, but it will certainly trouble an opponent if it is close enough to the side, and it will also give you time to recover to the centre of the court, if that is the object of playing the lob.

HARD-HIT SHOTS

The final pair of shots to make up the eight are the hard-hit shots. These are much more difficult to describe, as they cover a much wider bracket than any of the other three pairs. One drop shot is pretty much like another drop shot, and angles all have a good deal in common, but I am now talking about anything from a firm drive to the back of the court to the fiercely struck cross court kill into the nick. However, the

1. Correct position for lob service: well forward in the service box, and the ball to be struck close to the side wall. Note the foot position – a line through the toes leads to the point on the front wall where the stroke is being aimed

Correct position for defensive ̄ice. Ball about to be struck over ̄re of court position as a backhand ̄ aimed to return close to the her side wall

3a. (*Left*) Return of service: correct position for the beginner. Close to the back wall to judge length of ball, eyes on server to gain maximum anticipation time, and ready to move forward into the 'triangle' to intercept the good service at a convenient spot. 3b. (*Right*) A good service has hit the side wall high, and is just coming into the triangle area. Hand out must now take it and volley it, firm-wristed, down the side wall

3c. (*Left*) Hand out has moved up to the tip of the triangle to cut off a high service; he is volleying with a firm wrist, and will follow through with the racket held high. The ball will return down the side wall. 3d. (*Right*) *Wrong:* Hand out has gone outside his triangle, and is trying to hit the ball at the most difficult moment, instead of moving back to take it off the wall (as in 3b) or forward to cut it off before it gets there (as in 3c)

3e. The high volley played badly. The follow through has come down and across the line of flight, and almost certainly hit the ball into the tin. Note also wrong foot position, inevitably resulting in a shot across court

3f. The 'fly-swat'. The ball has been flicked at with a loose wrist, which will be more likely to hit the ball into the roof or floor than produce an accurate shot

4a. Retrieving from the back corners. Player's feet are facing the opposite side wall, his weight is on his right foot, and he is able to take a full swing, clear of the back wall

4b. The swing continues, with the wrist still 'locked', so that, at the moment of impact, the racket head can be flicked forwards and upwards, and the ball 'boosted' onto the side wall

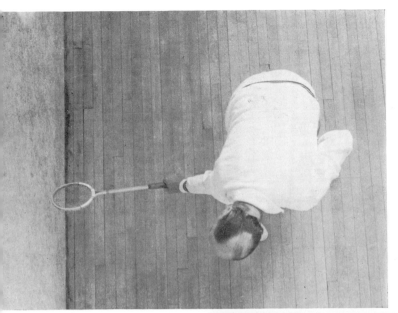

4c. The ball has been struck, and the follow through continues, as the player straightens upwards. Note that the racket head has now 'overtaken' the wrist

4d. The end of the follow through. The player is now upright, and the racket has continued to swing upwards. The feet are still in position, and the player is on balance

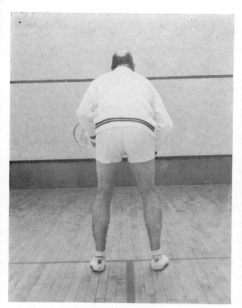 

5a. (*Left*) Elementary tactics. 'Blinkers': the player is gazing at the front wall, waiting eagerly for the ball to arrive in his arc of vision. He will be slow to move to any shot, but will be particularly suspect to the drop or the hard hit down the wall.

5b. (*Right*) Correct position on 'T' – no 'blinkers' here. Player is watching the ball right on to his opponent's racket, and is on balance, prepared to move in any direction

5c. The 'Oak tree'. The player in the front backhand corner has just played a poor lob, and his opponent, correctly placed on the 'T', is preparing to hit a very likely winner into the back forehand corner

6a. (*Top*) Poised to play any of the eight possible shots, and ready to amend the choice at the very last moment, if the opponent can be heard moving in any particular direction. 6b. (*Centre*) In a rally where most of the shots have been hard strokes up and down the forehand wall, the player in the front is varying this with an angle to the front backhand corner, as his opponent begins to move in anticipation of another drive. 6c. (*Bottom*) Previously, the player on the right has hit the ball from this position as a hard drive into the back backhand corner. His opponent is anticipating this again, but the player has in fact played a hard reverse angle, which will end up in the front forehand corner, the furthest point from the anticipated position

7a. The reverse angle. In position to play any stroke

7b. The ball is hit early, and the wrist helps to flick it across the court. The body shields the stroke from the opponent on the 'T', who therefore cannot anticipate it

7c. Note how, even in this wide cross-court shot, the follow through has come up and not across, and is not endangering an opponent who may have guessed wrong and come too close. Notice also the balance, and the eye still on the ball

8a. Retrieving the 'clinger'. When a ball is clinging to the side wall the only sure way to return it is to make your racket also cling to the wall, going in the opposite direction. Hit the racket reasonably gently on the wall with a loose wrist, and then use the wrist to flick the racket forwards and upwards along the wall

8b. The end of the shot. The racket has followed through upwards; the upward movement is necessary to ensure that the ball will carry to the front wall, as the shot cannot be struck hard without risk of breaking the racket!

9a. (*Left*) Stroke play – the backhand drop shot. Backswing as for any other stroke, in order not to reveal intention, and to enable last-minute change of stroke to be effected. 9b. (*Right*) Note: eye on ball, racket head well up, legs and body bent to allow stroke to be played with racket horizontal, weight on front foot, ball struck level with front foot, and racket face 'open' to take speed off the ball and 'guide' it just above the tin

9c. A complete follow through, upwards rather than around and across court, and eye still on the ball

10. Penalty point to the player in the back of the
court. His opponent has played a poor shot, and is
now vulnerable to the direct hit, which would lose
him the point, as it would be going straight to the
front wall. If the player refrains from playing the ball,
he must nevertheless be awarded the point

11a. Penalty point. Player on the right has played a poor shot back towards himself. As his opponent approaches, he must move away towards the side wall or the back of the court, and enable his opponent to attempt a drop or angle winner in the front of the court

11b. The player has refused to move clear and give his opponent freedom of stroke, and must be penalised

12a. Player on the 'T' has hit a good reverse angle and his opponent is desperately trying to scrape it up. The player is beginning to follow up, to be in position to kill the return

12b. The opponent has scraped the ball up somehow, but his momentum has carried him forward, so that he is blocking the player behind him from the ball, and the winner to back of the court. Point to the player

13a. Penalty point. Player is aiming to play a length shot down the wall, forcing his opponent to move to the back backhand corner, and leaving a clear path back to the 'T' position for himself

13b. Player has mishit the shot and it is returning along a line between his original position by the wall and the 'T'. In his movement back to the 'T' he clearly obstructs his opponent's view of the ball and stroke at it. Point must be awarded to the opponent

13c. No penalty! Having played his poor shot, the player has refrained from backing across the 'T', and is allowing his opponent freedom to attempt a winning stroke: in this case, an angle shot into the front forehand corner

14a. (*Right*) No let situation. Player in rear of court has played a poor stroke back to his opponent's 'Oak tree'. He must now give his opponent complete freedom to attempt a winner, and his only hope is to move very quickly up the court, around one side or the other of his opponent, and hope that he can get to the ball

14b. (*Left*) Player on the 'T' has now struck the ball and opponent has committed himself to moving up on forehand side. He can only hope that the ball has gone to that side, or been hit so inaccurately to the backhand that he can get across to it. If the shot is a winner, it is the fault of the defending player's previous weak shot

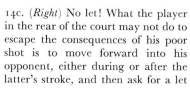

14c. (*Right*) No let! What the player in the rear of the court may not do to escape the consequences of his poor shot is to move forward into his opponent, either during or after the latter's stroke, and then ask for a let

15. No let situation. The last time the player in front was in this position he played a straight drop shot. His opponent, remembering this, has moved up to anticipate, only to find that the player has wrongfooted him with an angle. He cannot now claim that he has not had a fair view of the ball

16a. Correct movement from the ball. The player in the front of the court is about to play a drop shot, and his opponent is moving up in anticipation

16b. Having played his drop, the player has correctly moved towards the centre of the court before moving back to the 'T', and has given his opponent a clear run at the ball. Had he moved straight back to the 'T' or down the wall and then across, he could hardly have avoided obstructing. The same rule applies in the back corners

basics still hold good; the ball should be approached as usual, the feet in the same place and the racket swing in the usual groove. The intention will vary with the speed of the ball, the state of the match and, more than with any of the other shots, the player's own ability. Some people have the knack of hitting the ball hard and well, others have not, and up to a point, it is not something that can be developed. If a beginner finds that he does not naturally hit the ball hard, he should not worry about it, or in trying to do so he will merely develop a huge follow through and injure some- one.

However, it is necessary to be able to hit the ball hard enough, to play a winner, if the opponent is out of position and you have an open space to exploit before he can recover. Most rallies are played at a good pace, and the normal bread-and-butter shots, while waiting for an opening for a winner, are firmly hit strokes down the side walls. There is one vital difference between these shots and lobs: the cross court lob goes over the oak tree area, and should strike the back wall near the rear corner, but if a firmly hit shot fol- lowed the same path it would go straight into the opponent's oak tree area. So any cross court shot must be hit wider, to pull the opponent away from the 'T' to the further wall; but even then there is the danger that he may get there in time to hit it crisply down that wall, while you are still the other side of the court. So hard hit shots across the court are very dangerous; really, I feel that they should be kept for situations where you know that your opponent is out of position, and the cross court area is safe. If he is on the 'T', it is asking for trouble.

One word of warning: although it will seem to you as though every squash player you see is hitting every shot just as hard as he can, this is only the equivalent to every young cricketer going through the stage of wanting to be a fast bowler! It is important to try to speed your opponent up, and you can only do this by putting the ball where he is not, and for about half the time this will call for a soft shot. If you hit hard too often, you will not only find it tiring, but will also make it easy for your opponent to anticipate your shots; and if you hit too hard for your own accuracy, you will find that you are merely giving him the ball to hit again, before you have had time to get to the 'T'. It is very easy to find that a rally is getting faster and faster, and you are losing control of it; it is rather like running down a hill, and eventually being unable to stop without coming to an almighty crash. The way to avoid being hurt was, when you realised the danger, to sit down, and the time to regain control of a rally is when you realise it is going too fast for you; hit a good high lob, take a deep breath, gather your thoughts on the way back to the 'T' and go on from there. Never try to hit yourself out of trouble; for every occasion you get a lucky shot past your opponent, there will be nine when he puts the ball well out of your reach, while you are still out of position.

MOVING AROUND THE COURT

So much for various strokes. In the next chapter I will give you various suggestions about how you can practise them. Before going on to that, I want to add a final word about movement around the court. I have said that after each stroke you must go back to the centre of the court as rapidly as possible, in order to 'plant your oak tree', but in doing so, you must keep clear of your opponent on his way to the ball, and you cannot just charge straight back to the 'T', if it involves the risk of sending him flying. It is always correct to circle back to the 'T' by the centre of the court route; this means that from whichever corner of the court you are in, your first movement should be towards the centre of the court and then up or down to the 'T'. It is wrong, and will lead you into trouble, either by obstructing your opponent, or by giving him wide open spaces to aim at, if you move up or down first, and then try to cross to the 'T'. It is even worse if you try and crawl along a side wall! And do remember that once you have played your shot, the onus is on you to give your opponent a fair view of the ball and complete freedom to play any stroke he wants to at it, whenever he likes, before it bounces for the second time.

6. Practice

Having discussed what the various shots are, we must now suggest ways in which to practise them. Ideally, there are two steps to be taken in order to perfect a stroke. To begin with, it is necessary to be able to produce the shot in the first place, and then to produce it in action. Before you can play a drop shot in the middle of a rally, having had to run several yards to the ball, you have to have the basic idea of what a drop shot is aiming to do, and the knowledge of the technique of actually playing it. Perhaps the best way of climbing these two rungs on the ladder of stroke production is to take the first step on your own and the second in company with a partner also keen to learn and improve the shots, which you wish to practise.

INDIVIDUAL PRACTICE
Firstly, then let us talk about individual practice. There are dangers in this, which it is wise to be aware of. For example, some people are much less mentally suited to practising on their own than others, and very quickly get bored with it, and need a partner to make them concentrate on the job in hand. Others can think they are practising shots in the right way, but because they have no coach with them, and not even a friendly partner to offer constructive criticism, they may not realise that in fact they are gradually getting into some very bad habits. There is also the danger, when one is practising alone, especially on cold courts, and when practising the softer shots like the drop or the lob service, that

the ball is allowed to get very cold, and well below the speed it would be during an actual game. The result is that the player gets, for example, a first-class lob service with that particular ball, but when he comes to reproduce it in a proper game, the ball flies into the roof, because it is much faster. Nevertheless, provided these dangers are borne in mind, there is a good deal of useful practice, which a player can put in on his own, prior to getting to work with a partner.

Basically, there are three things which can usefully be done alone. One is to learn to produce the various shots correctly, the other is to learn accuracy, and the third is speed and stamina practice and training. Let us look at these three things in turn.

I have described earlier in the book the basic stance and racket swing for all the strokes in squash, and in the last chapter, the eight possible shots. It is now up to you to go into court with a red or blue dot ball, and try these shots out. The best way to do so is to get into as easy a position as possible in the middle of the court, hit or throw the ball against the front wall, so that it comes back conveniently to the side of you that you intend, and then play the stroke you are practising. Do not drop the ball for yourself, because in an actual game the ball will be coming at you from the front wall, and so the only worth-while practice for a stroke is when it is played at a ball coming at you from this direction. It not only gets the shot going realistically, but gives the eyes practice at working out the approach and bounce of a moving ball, and the body practice at moving into the correct position to play the ball opposite the front foot, with the stance and swing correct. After you have played the stroke, remain in position and do a little self criticism. Was the shot a success or not, and did it feel right? Why did it go wrong, if it did, and so on. On your own you have time to do this sort of thing without wasting someone else's time, so make the most of it. Do remember, however, one of the dangers I mentioned; the one about letting the ball get cold. If you

69

are doing this rather leisurely and throughtful practice, even with a red or blue ball, keep it warm by banging it up and down on the floor, or hitting it hard a few times against the wall, if you are at a stage to do this.

As far as accuracy practice is concerned, this is certainly something a player can usefully do on his own. We said before that the basic shot in a squash rally is one up and down the side wall, and as close to it as possible. This is the most important 'accuracy' to learn, down the walls on both sides of the court. Like all practices, make it as easy as you can in the initial stages; you can do this by beginning well up the court and gradually moving back to the ideal place, which is just behind the rear line of the service box. You can set yourself a target of so many shots, all of which must return between you and the side wall, and as close to the wall as possible, and when you do get to the position near the back of the court, the ball should be causing problems because of its good length; remember that this is when a ball gets a player in two minds as to whether to play it before it gets to the back wall or wait for it to come back from it, and either is fraught with danger. So the ideal that one is aiming at is a shot actually clinging to the side wall all the way along, and dying in the back corner.

Perhaps this is a good moment, in passing, to give a little advice about how to pick a ball off a wall when it is very close to it. You see a lot of players shut their eyes and hope, and miss by a couple of feet, others have a panic-stricken jab at the wall, which happily combines losing the rally and costing several pounds worth of racket. The answer is to play an upward stroke with a loose wrist, deliberately hitting the wall just behind where you aim to hit the ball. The loose wrist will prevent a racket breaking on impact with the wall, and if the wrist then pushes the racket on, it will stay close to the wall and return the ball. Do not be afraid of hitting the wall in this way; the racket will take it, and you will soon lose your fear of this shot. Again, start easily by going near a wall, and very gently, in slow motion and without a ball, try the shot as I have just explained it, and gradually speed it up. It is never a hard-hit shot, but an upward one, as it is quite likely to hit the wood of the frame of the racket or be a semi-mishit, and the ball must be given the upward direction to carry it to the front wall.

SPEED AND STAMINA

There are many varieties of accuracy practice, especially as one gets more competent. The down the wall practice can be varied to include lobs as well as drives, volleys, high or low as well as ground strokes. Then all sorts of tasks can be set; for instance, a high lob down the wall could be answered by a hard overhead volley, also down the wall, which could lead to a high cross court lob and this could repeat the sequence on the other side of the court. Sequences can very easily be worked out to include all the various shots, and this leads on to the third type of solitary exercise, involving training in speed and stamina. In matches nowadays the rallies tend to be very long drawn out affairs, and players tend to be able to keep up their speed and wind during frequent rallies of fifty, eighty or a hundred shots. Matches may last up to two hours, and so fitness is important.

However, in a rally you are playing alternate shots, whereas in individual practice you are playing every shot. And when you are on your own, you can cheat as much as you like, and get the ball back on the eighth bounce, if you want to. So set yourself a time limit, or a shot limit, of three or four minutes, or 150 or 200 shots, and go as hard as you can for that time, regardless of whether you got the ball up or not. You will find it very tiring, and you will not be able to do many sessions of this at one time. But you will gradually be able to increase the number of these bursts of frenzied activity that you can include in your practice periods, mixed in with the other things we have already mentioned. A happy mixture is a good idea, because there is no point in being able to play all the shots perfectly, but being too fat, slow or idle to get to the ball in time to play them; there is no point in being tremendously fit and fast and getting to the ball with bags of time to spare, if you are then going to miss it or hit it in the tin!

However, there is a third ingredient, which individual practice can never supply, and that is hitting a ball, which someone else has hit at you, and hitting it back where it will be most difficult for him. So sooner or later, when you have learned how to produce all the shots, have improved your accuracy and your fitness, you are going to have to get a friend to come on court and provide the opposition, even if you are in fact, at first, simply practising the shots in pairs, as opposed to the individual practice you have just done.

PRACTISING WITH A PARTNER

Practice in pairs is a much more realistic thing; no longer do you know exactly where the ball is going to be hit, or how hard, and of course you now have another body in the court to keep clear of. What I hope to do is to suggest one way in which all the various shots can be practised by pairs of players; there are many other ways, which your coaches may be able to suggest, or which you can think up for yourselves, which are every bit as good as these, but at least you will have one little practice game for each shot. Do remember three things: firstly, that both players involved must have an equal amount of time at the things being practised; for instance, if you are practising service and the return of service, remember to change roles half-way through. Remember, also, to practise from both sides of the court; it is stupid to do nothing but go on lobbing from the front forehand corner, while the other person plays boasts from the back backhand corner. It is just as vital to practise lobbing from the backhand and boasting from the forehand. And thirdly, remember that you must return to the 'T' between shots in most of the exercises, because, although you may know for certain in the practice session that your opponent is going to hit the ball to a certain front corner for you to lob, and could therefore stand and wait for it, you are practising for a match, when you will be on the 'T', not knowing where the ball is going next, and will then have to move up to the corner to lob. So a very vital part of most of these practice rallies is the movement to and from the 'T', which will be essential when games begin in earnest.

One other point which I think is important, is that it makes serious practices much more enjoyable, as well as realistic, if they can be made competitive. I have, therefore, tried to include ideas for doing this, but of course it depends very much on how long individual pairs want to devote to any particular piece of practice how they decide to score it. So devise your own ways of making your practices competitive, and I think you will enjoy them more.

Let us now consider the two most important shots in any rally, the service and the return of service. Only too often one sees even the very best players simply stroll into the box, hitting the ball in the vague general direction of the opposite back corner, and merely get the rally started somehow. It is of course true, that on the hot courts on which most of the major championships are played, it is too much to hope that one will be able to produce an actual ace service; just as in the higher levels of chess it is too much to hope for a 'fool's mate' in four moves. But the chess masters do not casually stick any old pawn or knight vaguely down the board, just to get the game started. Their initial moves are deliberately thought out, and are intended to build the foundations for future attack from a sound defensive position. Squash, which is a physical form of chess played fast, should be the same. Care should be taken about the service, and it should be as attacking a shot as possible, but at the same time, a safe one. At the end of a close, five game match, I wonder how often the loser stops to consider that, if only he had really bothered about serving well, he might at least

73

have gained the initiative in several more rallies than he did, and so have been able to win them a few shots later, and have swung the match his way. Usually, I fear, he will be blaming his bad luck, the referee, the ball and his state of health, and it will never occur to him that it was his own fault.

At a lower level, when services can more often be aces, or force a weak return, it is obvious that it is the duty of every player not only to serve well, but also to have a safe return of service. It does not matter very much if one player has brilliant drops shots, or the other fabulous angles, if the rally never actually gets going. So do make room for service practice in your time tables.

Each player should have 20 consecutive services in turn, serving from alternate sides, exactly as he would in a match. If he serves, and Hand out does not return the ball, either because it is a great service or the return was a mishit, it is a point to the server. If it is returned, so that the server cannot get it up, it is a point to Hand out; if Hand in does play a correct third shot in the rally, it is a draw. Thus, at the end of his 20 services, Hand in might be winning by 4 service winners to 3 winning returns, with 13 draws, and Hand out then takes over for 20 services, and tries to beat a credit balance of 4–3. This practice ensures that the server moves correctly to the 'T', and that he watches behind him, as he would normally have to do. The 20 services give him scope for variety, but also time to concentrate on his best type of service on that court. Similarly, this practice forces Hand out to concentrate on watching the server, on moving forward into his 'triangle' and on trying to make winners off any loose services. It also keeps the ball warmed up.

The next practice game I want to suggest is one which concentrates on angles in the front of the court. So many people come to squash from other sports, where they lose the rally if they hit the ball anywhere but more or less straight ahead, and these people simply never consider deliberately hitting the ball on to a side wall; it is against every instinct that they have developed concerning racket games. And so one has to break down this barrier somehow, and how better to do it than by playing a series of rallies in which the only 'legal' shots are angles or reverse angles? So go with your partner into the front half of the court, and play rallies, each of which scores one point, in which every shot must hit a side wall on its way to the front wall, either as a straight or a reverse angle. The game can go on up to 9 or 15 points, as time allows, and is a very enjoyable little exercise. It has three main advantages; firstly, it forces the reluctant 'angler' to play these shots; secondly, it gives him the chance of watching his opponent playing them continually at close quarters, so that he will see the build-up to the shot, and this will perhaps help him to anticipate it better, when a genuine opponent does the same thing in a match; and thirdly, it gives both players very valuable experience in keeping out of each other's way in the front of the court.

When you and your partner have done enough angle practice, this game can be adapted for practising drop shots played in the front of the court. It just is not possible for you both to practise drops at the same time; if you try, you will end up in a very nasty heap in one of the front corners! The only way is if one plays drops towards the side wall, and the other 'opens' the court up again by playing an angle.

Most of the other shots can be practised in variations of a 'Front of the court versus Back of the court' game. One player is given the role of 'lobber', and he has to lob from, say, the front forehand corner into the back backhand corner; his partner is given the role of 'boaster', and he has to boast the lobs from the back corner out towards the front again, where the lob is repeated. Normally, of course, one only plays the boast out of the back corner when forced to do so by a particularly good length lob or drive, but in this practice the player at the back does it every time, whether forced to or not, in order to perfect the mechanics of the shot.

In order to make this practice effective, two things have to be borne in mind. Firstly, it must be remembered that not only must each player have his turn at the two roles, but also that the shots must be exercised from both sides of the court; that is to say, that half-way through one player's session in the front of the court he must change to backhand lobs into the rear forehand corner, and his partner must then switch to boasting from there, and when this has been done, the player who was in the back quarters has his turn at the front, and vice versa. Secondly, throughout this practice it is vital that both players return to the 'T' after each stroke.

All the exercises are ways of preparing people for match play, and it is not much use a coach allowing pupils to stand in a corner of the court and play shots from a static position; part of the practice, and a very important part too, is to give them experience in moving up to the ball, getting the feet and balance right, producing the shot, and then returning to the 'T'. You and your partner can try to make sure that this is done correctly by slipping in a surprise shot, very occasionally, if one suspects that the other is not moving back to the 'T'. The one in front can try a drop, instead of the usual lob; if the other person is on the 'T', he will either get to it, or be near to doing so. If he has hung around the back corner, waiting for the lob, it will be very obvious! Similarly, the one in the back of the court can sometimes play a surprise length shot down the side wall, and this will sort out whether the lobber has been coming back to the 'T', and incidentally, whether he is watching the ball behind him.

This practice can be built up to include more than the lob and boast; when the player in the front of the court has done his lobbing to everyone's satisfaction, he can switch to driving down the nearest side wall to as good a length as possible; with his partner still playing the boasts; he will then find himself driving down each side wall in turn, and the partner boasting from each rear corner in turn, which introduces more movement into the practice than was the case when it was lob and boast. When the rear player wants a change, he may, from then on, try to play straight drops from the back of the court, unless his partner forces him to boast by a particularly good length drive or lob.

Eventually, this practice can be built up so that the player in front is playing lobs, drives or any combination of length shots into the rear corners, while the other player is playing boasts or drops from the back of the court. Make sure, however, that you build the practice up into this multi-shot combination via good periods of time on the various component parts. Unless you do this, it is human nature for you and your partner to concentrate on the shots that you do best, and the weak strokes that really need the practice will not get it. So stick to times for whatever bits of this practice you are going to do on that day with your partner, and do not start off with a free-for-all.

HANDICAPPING

One of the peculiarities of squash is that a player only very slightly better or worse than his opponent will either beat him or lose to him by a very decisive score. This can make normal games between two players of differing levels of skill rather a waste of time; the better player becomes over-confident, careless and justifiably sure that a few points lost by stupid shots can soon be pulled back, and the weaker player feels that he has a hopeless task, and that whatever he does, his opponent will be able to turn on the heat, if and when he needs to, in order to win. So a normal game between the two with normal scoring is not a success, and in fact may do actual harm to both. There are, however, two types of handicap, which can enable players of very different standards to play together without either feeling that he is wasting his time.

First of all, do not ever enforce any 'unnatural' handicap on the better player, such as banning certain shots, barring certain areas of the court, making him carry heavy weights or lashing his ankles together. Things like this would do his squash no good at all, and even if they gave the other chap more chance of winning, he would not derive much satisfaction from a win under these conditions. As in all the practice games, we are rehearsing for actual matches, and the nearer we can get to the atmosphere and damands of a genuine game the better, and both of the games I am going to suggest are played exactly as an ordinary match would be played, and yet both partners are able to play flat out, despite their differing abilities, without either of them feeling that it is a waste of time.

In the first game, the play proceeds absolutely normally except that the better player only scores when he brings off a service ace. This can be because of a brilliant service or a poor return, but he can only get a point if Hand out does not return the service. If the service is returned, the rally is played out completely normally; if Hand out, the weaker player, wins it, he takes over service in the usual way, and has his chance of scoring a point if he can win the following rally too. If Hand in wins it, he continues his hand, serving in the normal way from the other service box, but the score remains the same. Thus, the stronger player really has to bother about his service, because it is the only way he can score, and this is good for his service; he then has to play the rally seriously, because he dare not risk losing it, and allowing his opponent to get in and perhaps sneak a lucky point. The weaker player, although obviously losing most of the rallies, has not got a hopeless task; he only has to return the service, and he cannot lose! This does wonders for his ability to get back even the most hostile services, and of course nothing improves anyone's play more than battling against someone better. He will be doing just that throughout the game, without feeling that it is all in vain.

The second suggestion, which again combines completely normal squash with giving each player an incentive all the time, is to play a game in which the stronger player scores a point for each game he wins, and the weaker scores every point. Thus, after four normal games the stronger player might be winning 9–0, 9–1, 9–0, 9–2, which would give him a lead in the overall game of 4–3. Again, at all times, both players have to go flat out; even if the stronger player is ahead at 8–0 in a game, he dare not relax and risk letting his opponent in, and even at 0–8 down, the weaker player still has the chance of getting in and collecting the one point he needs to break even on that game.

As far as tournaments are concerned, the more normal types of handicap are by awarding points, either plus or minus, by giving the weaker player a 'hand' or more, which means that when he has become Hand in, his opponent has to win more than the usual one rally to take over the service again, and by allowing the weaker player American scoring, which means that he scores a point for every rally he wins, whether Hand in or out at the time. These methods of handicapping, which can be used separately or combined with each other, can be used for practice, but only when the difference in playing standard is slight, and there is a danger in them, which is apparent when one does see a handicap tournament in progress, that the better player tends to feel compelled to play defensive squash, which is the last thing one wants to encourage, especially in practice, where the accent should be on improving strokes.

DEFENSIVE PLAY

Nevertheless, the last type of game that I want to suggest to you as being a good training for a genuine match, is the one which does exercise defensive play. There is a danger, if this is not done sometimes, of players going into a match with no thought in their minds beyond flashing around the court, dazzling their opponent and a packed gallery with a continual stream of the brilliant strokes they have been practising. This is fine, if it happens to be an occasion when the court allows you to lob well, when the speed of the ball is right for your strokes, when your eye is in and all the shots are working well, and when your opponent is allowing you just enough time to be in position and on balance to play them with confidence. It is not so good, when you find yourself on a court with a low roof, when you have a very fast ball, your timing is out, because you have a splitting headache, and your opponent is rushing you all over the court. Certainly under these conditions, and even in a normal game, there come moments when a player cannot afford to lose another point. This might be when the games are one all, and one player is losing the third game 6–3. At this stage the flashy cross court half volley drop, which was working so well a week ago, is an expensive luxury, which you cannot afford.

This is the moment to switch into defensive gear, and determine not to run any risks whatever. Make up your mind that at least you are not going to lose any points, until the situation changes, and you are going to make it as hard as possible for your opponent to win them. This means that you are going to return every shot safely, without trying any touch shots that could go wrong, and by playing the ball continually into the back corners of the court, frequently down the side walls and as close to them as possible, you will not risk setting up any winners. In fact, you hope that your opponent, so near to winning the game, and perhaps feeling that his lead permits him the luxury of a few ambitious shots, may hit a few down through over confidence, and a desire to finish the game off quickly. Your aim must be to give him every chance to make these mistakes, make him frustrated and see the game he thought he had won gradually slipping away.

It is also a good idea to do this at the start of a match, and indeed at the start of each game. Nerves can play a part at those moments, and it is wiser to get the feel of the ball by playing unglamorous, safe, length shots and lobs, and hope to build up a lead, than to play a series of risky attempts at winners. If you can get a lead, then it can be used as a little fat to live on, while you get all your shots working, and it means that you are in the commanding position.

So the practice game is simply one in which one player restricts himself completely to lobs, across court or down the walls, and drives down the walls, with the aim of forcing the opponent to take the ball continually either very close to the side wall, or right in the back corners. The other player is allowed complete freedom to play any shots he wishes, and of course after one game in these roles, they change over. Not only is this good practice for the person playing the defensive game, but it is also excellent practice for the other person, who has to try and work out how best to play against it, because sooner or later he will run up against someone in a match who will be doing just that, and he must have worked out his own ways of trying to break it up, maintain pressure and yet not take unjustified risks.

To sum up my ideas on practice, then, I would say that there is nothing better than actual matches, whether you win or lose them, provided that you learn from them. Individual practice is fine, if you have a definite aim in view and have the sort of mentality that can discipline yourself to carry out tasks on your own. Practice with a partner can be most helpful, and it makes it more interesting, if this can be made competitive. Make your practice realistic, and above all enjoyable. If it becomes a chore, you will soon get fed up, both with the practice and with squash !

7. The Advanced Rules

So far we have only discussed the very basic rules in squash; just enough for beginners to play games correctly, and keep the score. It does not take long, however, for people, who are learning the game, to run into situations, which need a good deal more explaining than that. As we said in Chapter One, squash is like tennis, but with both players on the same side of the net, and it is this fact, which requires many extra rules not needed in games where a net separates the opponents. The rules have to cope with one of the players being hit with the ball, and the even more difficult situation, when there is physical obstruction and the rally comes to an untimely end because there has been a collision, or one player cannot see or get to the ball because of his opponent's position.

Because of this 'physical contact' side of squash, a good deal of 'needle' can creep into a match, unless it is being properly and firmly controlled, and in a top match there should be a Marker and a Referee. It is quite unfair to expect players to make their own decisions, as both must be biased, and neither is really able to judge the other's speed or direction. However, before anyone can help players by offering to mark or referee games, they must know thoroughly the rules they are going to administer. Furthermore, because most players come to squash from other sports, and it is an easy game to pick up and become quite good at, many very experienced players do not have a proper grounding in the rules.

WHEN A PLAYER IS HIT WITH THE BALL

Let us now consider these more advanced rules, which will not only help people learning to play the game, but will also lead into the next chapter, where we discuss how markers and referees should carry out their tasks. And, first of all, I will explain the rules that apply when a player hits his opponent with the ball.

If he hits him when the ball is on its way to the front wall, then there are three possibilities: if the ball was going directly to the front wall, and would have been a good return, it is the striker's rally; if it was going to be a good return, but going via a side wall, or even the back wall, then a 'let' is allowed (i.e. the rally is restarted on level terms), and if the ball was not going to be a correct return anyway, the rally is awarded to the person, who has been hit.

In the second case, where the let is allowed, it does not matter whether the opponent is hit with the ball between the striker's racket and the side wall, or between the side and front walls. The thinking behind the rule is that, if a player is directly in front of his opponent, he is 'baulking' him, and not giving him freedom of stroke, and thus if he is hit, it is his fault that the rally has ended, and so deserves to lose it. If, however, a player has given his opponent freedom to play the ball to the front wall, but is struck by a more ambitious, and therefore less easy to anticipate and avoid, shot, it is neither player's fault, and it is fair to play the rally again. Thirdly, if a player fails to play a correct return, it is wrong that he should be able to replay the rally just because the ball had happened to touch his opponent.

As always in the rules of squash, however, there are exceptions to the rules to provide the fair answer to unusual cases, where a rigid application of the letter of the law would prove harsh. There are two cases where a 'let' is awarded, even though one player hits his opponent with the ball, which was going direct to the front wall as a good return. The first is when the player has 'turned' on the ball. By 'turning' I mean the action of following the ball round, usually in the back corner of the court, and taking it as a forehand in the backhand half of the court, and vice versa. Normally this happens when the player has tried to cut the ball off, but found it too high, fast or close to the side wall to do this, and has then chased it round and retrieved it after turning a full circle. Usually, the ball will have hit the side and back walls, but it need not have done so, and this rule applies to any instance where a player follows the ball round and then hits his opponent.

The reason why only a let is given in this case is because it is quite impossible to anticipate the direction of this shot, and so it is not reasonable to penalise a player if he is struck by it. The second instance is when a player has played a stroke at the ball, but has missed it; if he then recovers in time to play a further shot at the ball, and gets it up, but hits his opponent as the ball heads straight for the front wall, this too is only a let. The reasoning is similar; the opponent was presumably clear of the first stroke, and could hardly be expected to guess that the player was going to achieve an 'air' shot, and that he himself was in danger of being hit by a second attempt. Once again, a let is the fair result to the situation.

So much for cases in which a player hits his opponent with the ball as it is on its way to the front wall. If he hits him as his shot returns from the front wall then, in normal circumstances, it is his point, on the grounds that his opponent has been too slow to get his racket to the ball, has missed it, or was too off balance to play a stroke and avoid being hit. Once again, if there are extenuating circumstances, a let can be allowed. Such cases cover situations in which it is not entirely the other player's fault that he has been hit. For instance, if a player mishits the ball in such a way that it comes back directly towards him, and he then leaps out of the way, so that the ball hits his opponent, who was standing behind him and has had no fair view of the ball, then clearly the opponent can hardly be penalised. The same would apply in a case where the two players were close together, and as the ball approached, the position of the striker's body prevented his opponent from moving clear of the approaching ball, and he was struck as a result. Thus, in these instances, as in all others, the rule is trying to ensure that the fair result to each situation is achieved; it covers the most usual case, but has outlets for the less usual, so that no player is unfairly penalised.

Finally, there is the rule which covers the case of a player being struck by his own shot as it returns from the front wall. Normally, he will lose the rally, but again, there can be cases when he would get away with a let. For example, it would be unfair to penalise him if the opponent was standing too close and was actively preventing him from moving clear of the approaching ball. Or if the opponent shaped up to play a shot, then decided to let it go through to the back wall, and the ball hit the original striker. Similarly, if the opponent actually plays a shot and misses the ball, and it goes on to hit the player, it would be hard on the latter to rule that he ought to have assumed the other person was going to miss, and have jumped aside! Once again, the rule has its escape clauses for the unusual case.

OBSTRUCTION

Now let us consider the very difficult question of penalising a player for obstruction. The rule *requires* – note the word : not 'hopes', 'expects' nor 'encourages', but requires – a player, when he has completed his stroke to do everything in his power to give his opponent a fair view of the ball, and freedom to play the ball to any part of the front wall, or the side wall near the front wall. It is important to be quite clear what the rule says on this point; the final part of Rule 17 Para (iii) states: 'if in the opinion of the referee a player has not made every effort to comply with these requirements of the rule, the referee shall stop play and award a stroke to his

85

opponent.' Of course, if play has already stopped, the referee has to 'award the stroke' in the same way, but again the wording is vital. 'The referee shall' is an order; it is not a suggestion that he 'may' give the rally to the innocent party, and thus the rule is very definitely insisting that players must keep out of the way or be penalised.

However, it sometimes happens that even when a player is genuinely doing his best to get out of the opponent's way, he may be unable to do so, perhaps because he is off balance, or has mishit his own shot, so that he is too close to it. If this happens, and as a result he prevents his opponent from making a winner, the referee may still award the rally to his opponent. Thus there are two types of penalty point; the first is for deliberate obstruction, when the offending player has not 'made every effort' to give his opponent fair view and freedom of stroke, regardless of whether the latter had a likely winner lined up or not, and the second for accidental obstruction, when the opponent did have a winner on, and was prevented from attempting it.

This rule has always been a problem, and still is. When squash was simply a friendly form of exercise between two people playing for fun, no such legislation was necessary, and as a result, when competition increased, and it was necessary in everyone's interest to cater for the ruthless player, the idea developed that awarding a point against someone was the equivalent of calling him a cheat. This is ridiculous. Even so, many experienced players, and even referees, still look on these decisions as insulting and unnecessary, and award lets where it is quite clear that the rules require a point to be awarded. My own view is that a pleasant player will not wish to profit from a situation in which he has, quite unintentionally, prevented his opponent from playing a winner, and will thus accept the referee's award of the rally to his opponent with a good grace, and the ruthless player must not be allowed to profit from it. A referee should award the rally to the innocent player with as little compunction as he does when the ball hits the tin or the out of court line; it is just another way of losing a rally.

The rule about deliberate obstruction must be enforced at any time that the referee considers it necessary, in any part of the court, and he must not fail to do so, because, for one thing, the safety of the opponent may be at stake, and any injury that results from a player being allowed to crowd persistently will be the referee's fault.

The accidental obstruction situations, however, fall into three main categories. When a player has a probable winning shot lined up, it is either the result of a previous good shot on his own part, which has induced a weak reply just waiting to be put away, or a poor shot on his opponent's part which has given him the chance of a kill. In either case, justice demands that he be given the chance to try and play his winner, and if the other player inadvertently prevents him from attempting to cash in, then it is quite unfair to start that rally again on level terms. The first of the three categories is when a player has played a good shot to the front of the court; the opponent just manages to scrape it up, but is off balance and unable to move sufficiently clear of his own shot to allow the original player to hit the obvious winner to the back of the court. It is just that the first player be awarded the rally, as though his opponent had failed to get the ball up; it would be unjust to have a let and start the rally again.

The second category is at the back of the court: if a player hits a poor shot more or less back towards himself, he must then do all he can to allow his opponent to play whatever shot he wishes. It may mean that he has to back away, even into the rear corners of the court, because it will clearly be in his opponent's interest to take the ball as late as he can, if by so doing he can force the player to the back wall, and then play a drop or angle winner to the front of the court. Again, justice decrees that the person who has played the bad shot must give his opponent his chance to cash in on it. If the rule did not exist it would simply mean that, every

87

time a player mishit a stroke and gave his opponent an advantage, he would deliberately run into the opponent and get a let. This, of course, a ruthless player may still do, if the referee allows him to get away with it!

The final category is the most frequent, and perhaps the hardest to judge fairly. It occurs when a player jumps across the line of the ball, when it is his own shot on its way back from the front wall, and therefore his opponent's turn to hit it. It usually occurs when a player is quite near a side wall, and in mid-court. His aim is to hit a length shot down the side wall, with the ball passing between himself and the wall. However, he mishits it, either by pulling the ball too far over on the front wall, or by hitting it into the side wall on its way to the front. Whichever it is, the result is that the ball is now coming back along a line which passes between himself and the 'T', where obviously he wishes to be. His opponent, presumably, is there, and is delighted to see the ball coming into his oak tree area, and is all set to play his winner into the wide open spaces on the other side of the court. However, just as he is lining up for the shot, and judging the speed of the approaching ball, there is a loud noise and a white shape hurtless across in front of him. The point is that the player who has set up this situation must not try to recover from it by leaping across to the 'T', if in doing so, he interferes with his opponent's fair view of the ball, or his stroke at it. Note the 'if in doing so': there is nothing in the rules condemning a movement across the line of the ball if no obstruction is caused, but if it is, the referee should penalise the obstructor.

The other situation which a referee should award a point is not strictly speaking a penalty point, but is closely related to one. It is when a player refrains from playing a shot, because he knows his opponent is in the way, and he does not want to hit him. If, in the referee's opinion, he would have won the point had he done so, because it would have been a stroke going direct to the front wall, the referee should award him the rally anyway. The thinking here is that a ruthless player will make sure of the rally by going through with the shot, regardless of whether he hurts his opponent, or introduces an unpleasant note into the match, and it is quite wrong that the pleasant player should lose out, simply because he is playing in a nicer way.

So, whenever a rally ends as a result of any obstruction, or indeed while a rally is still in progress and there is any obstruction going on in it, the referee has to decide whether to award a let or a point. Basically the difference is that he will award a let when he thinks it is fair to both players to restart the rally on level terms, and he will award one player the rally when he feels it would be unfair on him to do this, because he had a winning position which he had not been allowed to exploit, or because his opponent had infringed the rules.

OTHER STOPPAGES

A let is always given for any normal stoppage in play, such as the door coming open, anything falling in the court, which might distract or injure the players, or the ball breaking. It is not allowed if a player's racket breaks or his shoes split, or any other dramatic disaster happens to his clothing or person, however unlucky. It is hardly his opponent's fault if the rally has come to an end because his shorts are now round his ankles! Nor is it a let if the ball bounces in a odd way, or flies off a protruding door handle; this is just taken as the luck of the game, which might happen for or against either player. However, it might be as well to cover the situation concerning ball breakages and injuries.

When the ball breaks there is no specific time laid down in which the new one is warmed up; this is because conditions vary so much. If a match is taking place on a cold court in January, and new ball has to be fetched from a box in a cupboard, it might be necessary to knock it up for three or four minutes, before it reached anything like match speed, whereas on a hot court, when referee has had the good sense to have a spare in his pocket, a very few hits will be enough. Usually, the players agree between themselves, but the referee must make sure that neither player takes advantage of the incident unfairly. Sometimes the fitter of the two will try to rush his opponent into restarting before the ball is genuinely warmed up, and sometimes the more tired of the two will try and prolong the knock up, while he recovers a little more of his wind. The referee would clearly have to step in, if either was happening.

There are three types of injury, and each would be dealt with differently. The first is a self-inflicted injury : if a player breaks an Achilles tendon, or trips over his own feet and goes head first into a wall, and in either case cannot continue, he must concede the match, whatever the score might have been at the moment of disaster. At the other end of the scale is an injury caused, in the opinion of the referee, by one player against his opponent. This would almost certainly be as a result of a wild racket swing, although any form of physical assault would qualify. Certainly, if one player could not continue play through the culpable violence of his opponent, the referee would disqualify the opponent, and award the match to the injured player – posthumously if necessary!

However, between these two extremes, there lies the usual type of injury, where there has been a collision of some sort, with neither player more to blame than the other, as a result of which, one of them has emerged with a bad gash, or some other injury, requiring urgent medical attention. When this happens the injured player is given the maximum possible time to recover, even to the point of allowing the match to hang over to the next day, if conditions allow. If the player cannot continue even so, then he must concede the match; if he can begin again the same day, the game is resumed at the previous score as it was, when the injury took place. If the match has to wait until the following day, it is begun again at love all in the first game, unless both players agree to continue where they left off.

Now let us get back to lets. So far we have discussed the difference between lets and penalty points, but the referee has a third decision he can make, when a player asks for a let, and that is to refuse the request, and say 'No Let'. Basically, the referee will normally err on the generous side and award a player a let on request, if he thinks he had a chance of getting the ball up. He will only refuse the let, if he is absolutely certain that the player really had no chance of doing so, even if his opponent had been well clear. The reasoning here is that one is often amazed at squash by just what players can retrieve, and on these occasions, if the player had been obstructed, and asked for a let, it might have been refused; the fact that the ball was returned, to everyone's surprise, would show such a decision to be wrong. So a let will only be refused if it really is clear that the player could not have got to the ball.

The referee will, however, be less generous in situations where the player who is asking for the let is to blame for the situation that has occurred, usually because he has anticipated his opponent's stroke wrongly, and has, as a result, got completely out of position. For example, a player on the 'T' who assumes that his opponent, who is in one of the front corners, is going to play a drop, and comes up between the opponent and the side wall in an attempt to anticipate the shot and play an early winner off it, only to find that his opponent has fooled him by playing an angle, cannot then claim that he has not had a fair view of the ball. In fact, the only way he could get a let at all would be if the shot had not been a good one, and he had begun to move towards it, in the right direction now, at a speed which the referee considered sufficient to take him to the ball in time, if the opponent's body had not been in the way.

A similar instance of 'No Let' was one I had to give in an Amateur Championship match some years ago. A player, returning service from a back corner, decided to lob the ball over his opponent's head into the other back corner. However, as he hit the ball, he knew he had not hit it hard or high enough, and so he guessed that his opponent would try to play a 'stop' volley into the opposite front corner. The opponent might well have done so, had he not heard the player racing up the court. He therefore decided to hit the ball to a length into the back corner opposite to the one the player had just left. There was then a collision in the centre of the court, after which came an appeal for a let. This was clearly a case for refusing the let. After all, the person on the 'T' had given his opponent a clear run from his starting position to the position where the ball was, and if he chose to take a roundabout route, which caused a collision, he had only himself to blame.

It is also incumbent on a player to make very effort to get out of a bad situation that he has created, and he must not be allowed simply to run into his opponent and hope that a let will do this for him. You will sometimes see a player, who has played a bad shot straight to his opponent on the 'T', and who is now stuck behind the opponent, wait until the latter has played his shot, so that he cannot be guilty of crowding, but then run into him, instead of committing himself to one side or the other. In such a case, the referee should rule that it is no let, because the player is not going in a direct line to where the ball presumably is, in one of the front corners, and because it is not fair on the opponent that the rally should be begun again level.

CONTINUOUS PLAY

There is one other important rule which must be observed, and that is the one that requires play to be continuous.

Squash is a physical game, and a very tiring one, and the rules do not permit players to take rests to recover 'their wind or condition'. If a player can, by good retrieving, force his opponent into longer rallies than he can manage, or by good stroke play, make him run further than he wants, it is not fair that the opponent should be allowed to lean on the wall for a couple of minutes between rallies and recover. This is an obvious example, which the referee would clearly prevent, but it is less easy to stop the person who wears glasses from wiping them, the player whose shoe laces need continued attention, and the fellow who keeps 'accidentally' dropping the ball as he walks to serve, and has to stroll after it. The referee should warn these characters that, in his opinion, whether deliberately or not, they are wasting time, and should cease to do whatever it is, and in future make play continuous, as required by the rules.

So much for the rules themselves. Let us now go on to how they are administered by the Marker and Referee.

8. Marking and Refereeing

Having now discussed the rules in detail, it is necessary to see how they are administered and by whom. Ideally, every game of squash should have a Marker and Referee. More usually, in any except the very top level matches, one official does the two jobs, but even when this happens, it must be very clearly remembered that the roles of the two officials are completely different.

DIFFERENCE IN ROLES

The Marker is the person whose voice is heard calling the score, announcing when the ball is not up or out, and generally running the game. The Referee is in overall charge of the match, and is 'senior' to the Marker. All appeals go direct to the Referee and his decision is final, and he can of course use the final power of disqualification against any player whose behaviour warrants it.

The two officials should sit together in the centre of the front row of the gallery on a normal court, although new types of court, such as the glass-walled type, require special arrangements. It is important that they are together, because it is helpful to be able to discuss tricky situations during rallies, if either is unsighted, or for the Referee to be able to tell the Marker he is not spotting footfaults and so on. It is also much better to be in the centre of the gallery than on either side; wherever they sit, it is always possible that the players' bodies will conceal a double bounce or a ball touching the top of the tin, but by and large, the likelihood of this is less from a central position.

Let us now look at the duties of the two officials in detail. The Marker, whose voice keeps the game flowing, must do so by using the correct and accepted calls. Unfortunately, over the years, players have become suspicious of Markers, and more especially, Referees, because they have suffered from poor decisions from inexperienced officials, and they are only too ready to feel put off if the ones appointed for that particular match seem in any way to be unconventional. Quite unfairly, but understandably, they tend to bracket the ability of the two officials together, so that if the Marker begins calling odd or incorrect things, they automatically assume the the Referee is going to be suspect too. Conversely, if the game flows along in the generally accepted way, because the Marker is good, they will tend to have faith in the Referee. So, right from the very start, it is vital that the Marker makes the correct calls so that the players can get on with their game unworried, and in the frame of mind to accept the Referee's decisions.

The Marker and Referee will take their seats at the start of the knock up. After the correct period of five minutes the Referee will tell the Marker to call 'Time'. This call informs the players that they must now prepare to start the match. It is also used to indicate that the rest period between games is over, and play must restart, and either official may call 'Time' during a rally to stop play for any reason at all. So this call means 'Stop' what you are doing, and do something else! It is vital that players learn to stop at once when it is called during a rally; one of the reasons is to stop play when something has dropped into the court, or the door has opened, or anything else affecting the safety of the players has occurred. It may merely be because the players have not heard a call by the Marker of 'Not up', etc., and are playing on, or because the Referee wishes to award the rally to one of the players, or to warn one of them, but because of the danger possibility, the players must stop at once, if they hear 'Time' called.

THE MARKER

To go back to the start of the match, however, the Marker has called 'Time', and the players have removed their sweaters, have spun for service and are ready to start. The correct conventional way for the Marker to introduce the match is also the shortest : he announces the event, if it is worth introducing, by saying 'Final of the Blankshire Championship', then he announces the players, and which is which, by 'Smith serving, Jones receiving', followed by the terms of the match, which will probably be 'Best of five games' and lastly the score, which of course at that stage is 'Love all'. The call of the score then and throughout the whole match is the green light for Hand in to serve, and indicates that the Marker and Referee are ready to adjudicate the next rally. Provided that the service is a good one, the rally continues until one player fails to return the ball correctly, either by not getting to it before it has bounced twice on the floor (Marker calls 'Not up'), by hitting it into the tin (also 'Not up'), or by hitting it out ('Out of court'). It is generally acceptable for a Marker to call 'No' for any of these incorrect and rally-ending efforts, but the correct calls are as given.

However, the service may not have been correct. The types of crime that produce a double fault are called 'Out of Court', or 'Not up', as appropriate, but even more important is the correct calling of the single faults, because in that case, the call must be made early enough for Hand out to be able to make up his mind whether to take the ball or not. If it is a footfault, the Marker will call the word 'Foot-fault', in order to tell Hand in how he has erred, but for either of the other two types of single fault, the simple call of 'Fault' is made, as loudly, clearly, and above all, as early as possible.

At the end of the rally the Marker must call the score. If Hand in has won the rally, he merely adds one to that player's score, and as Hand in's score is always called first, what was, for example, 'One love' becomes 'Two love'. If, however, Hand in does not win the rally, the score remains the same, but is called the other way round, and so 'Two love' becomes 'Love two'. When this happens, the call of the score is preceded by the words 'Hand out', so the full score would, in this case, have been 'Hand out love two'. If Hand in needs only to win the next rally in order to win the game, the Marker adds the words 'Game Ball' to the call of the score; for example 'Eight two, Game Ball'.

If Hand in serves a single fault, and Hand out accepts it, the rally is in progress just as if the service had been good, and indeed Hand out has made the service good by the very act of taking it. If, however, a single fault is served and is not taken, the Marker should repeat the score before Hand in serves his second service, and add the words 'One Fault'. It is probably clear to Hand in at that moment that another single fault will lose him the service, but it is just possible that he may not have heard or registered the original call of 'Fault', and be under the impression that the ball has been returned to him because his opponent was not ready, and the call of 'One Fault' will make the situation quite clear. However, the importance of the call is for the situation when the second service has begun a rally which has ended in a 'let'. Because of the 'let', that rally never happened, so to speak, and we are back with the server restarting play with his second service. It is vital to remind him that he has one single fault chalked up against him, however many 'lets' there may be, until that particular point has been finally decided. If the let rally has been a long one, or there has been some debate with the referee over the let, it may well have slipped Hand in's mind that it all began with a single fault, and he will be 'Hand out' if he serves another.

And so the game proceeds with the Marker's calls as indicated until the game is over, unless the score reaches 8 all. At this moment, the Marker will call 'Eight all', and this is the cue for Hand out to elect 'No set' or 'Set two'. When he has indicated which it is to be, play continues up to 9 or 10 respectively until the game is won and lost. At the end of the game, the Marker calls 'Game to Smith', plus the score. He then waits for the Referee to instruct him to call 'Time', so that the players will know that the rest period is over, and the next game must begin. Before it does, the Marker will call 'One game to love', or whatever the score in games happens to be, and then 'Love all'. This system continues until one of the players manages to win the whole match.

That covers all the normal duties as far as the Marker is concerned, and the only other duty he has to do is to repeat any decisions of the Referee. Normally these will follow an appeal from one of the players for a 'let'; the appeal is a request from the player direct to the Referee, who will reply to the player, and the Marker then has to let everyone else know what that reply was, followed by the new score after the decision has been taken into consideration. There are three possible replies that the Referee can give to a request for a let – 'No let', 'Let Ball', or 'Point to Smith'. Remember, one always says 'Point to Smith', and never 'Point against Jones', and one never uses the phrase 'Penalty Point'. The reasons, of course, are to try to remove the stigma associated with the whole idea of the award of points, and to avoid any idea that one is criticising in any way the sportsmanship of the offending player. It is also possible for the Referee to bring a rally to an end at any time he thinks fit in order to award a let or a point, if he considers that this is the right and fair thing to do, and in these cases, too, the Marker must repeat the decision, plus the new score.

It all sounds very complicated at first, but in fact soon becomes a habit with practice. The easy way to remember the order in which things should be called is to realise that the first calls are things which affect the score in any way, the second are the words of the score itself, and finally, come any comments on the score. Thus, a complicated call like: 'Point to Smith, Hand out, Nine Eight, Game Ball' is made up as follows: the Referee has just made the decision to award the previous rally to Smith, and this will of course affect the score, and so it is called first. Then, as Jones had been serving at 'Eight Nine', and the score is now going to be reversed, the call of 'Hand out' is also necessary, as this too affects the order in which the numbers are called. The score itself is now 'Nine Eight'. Finally, 'Game Ball' warns Jones that he must be very careful not to lose this point, or the game goes as well.

This, then, is how a good Marker should 'call' a match, and I make no apology for mentioning again the point that it is vital for him to do his job correctly. His voice must be loud and clear, his calls the conventional ones, and he must work with his Referee, bearing in mind that it is the latter who has to make all the decisions.

THE REFEREE

Now for the Referee. It may well happen that he will have, apparently, nothing to do. So may a policeman, but he has always got to be ready at any moment to give advice, administer the law and act in an emergency. He has also to know his job, and to take every possible step beforehand to foresee any emergency. The Referee's duties, really start before the match even begins. Though it only applies in major events, he is strictly speaking responsible that the players do not practise on the match courts within an hour of the start of their match; he should know whether other courts would be available if, for any reason, the one in question become unplayable through condensation, lights failure, or any accident like some wall or ceiling collapse; he should know the whereabouts of first aid kit and how late the players could be allowed to play in the event of injury. However, even in a normal game, he should introduce himself to the players, tell them where he will be sitting, so they know which part of the gallery to look up at, when making any appeal, and should make sure that he and the Marker between them have an adequate supply of balls, and that seats have been reserved for them in the right place. It is no bad idea either to check that he and the Marker have watches with second hands, and pens or pencils in reserve, in case the ones in use to write down the score break during the game.

The Referee must then make sure that he is present for the start of the knock up. This is not just five minutes relaxation for him. Admittedly, his main concern will be to see that the permitted five minutes is not exceeded, but he has to keep an eye open for other things too. He should make sure that neither player is wearing black-soled shoes; he should make sure that the players are sharing the knock up fairly, and that neither is 'hogging' it and not giving his opponent an equal number of shots, and he should be having a look at the ball, in case either player claims it is too fast or slow, or is not bouncing truly, in which case he will have to adjudicate. At the end of the five minutes, he will tell the Marker to call 'Time', and when he has made sure that all illegally coloured clothing has been removed, and the door closed safely, he will allow play to start.

The one thing he must keep in his mind from the very first rally of the match until the last is that he is there for one reason, and one reason alone, which is to make sure that the fair and right result to that match is achieved, and the only way in which it can be achieved is if he ensures that the correct result to each rally is arrived at. He must, therefore, give exactly the same interpretation to the rule on lets and penalty points, and any other difficult situations, at every moment of the match; there must be no special leniency at love all in the first game or reluctance to end the match, by the award of a point at nine all in the fifth; his interpretations must be completely consistent. In the main, he will only be called upon to make decisions when there is an appeal from one of the players. He may, however, at any stage, stop play and award a let or a penalty point if he considers that this is the fair thing to do at that moment; or, at the end of a rally, he may again make an award even without an appeal.

Appeals come under two headings. The first, and most frequent, is for a let by a player who has not been able to return the ball, because of the obstruction, real or imagined, of his opponent. In this case the Referee has to decide whether to grant the let, refuse it, or award the player the point under the deliberate or accidental baulking rule that I explained in the last chapter. The second is an appeal against a call by the Marker. This can be because a player, whose shot has been called out or not up, thinks that it was in fact good, and wants the Referee to adjudicate. Alternatively, a player may appeal, because he thought that a shot by his opponent was not good, although the Marker appeared satisfied. In this instance, it must be remembered, that the player may well be appealing about a shot much earlier in the rally, and as a rally progresses, a Referee should make a mental note of shots about which he is either doubtful himself, or feels one of the players may be, so that he is aware of the shot referred to if there is an appeal.

Under these circumstances, the Referee must, as always, do his best to get the fair result to the rally. If he was sure the Marker was in error, he may overrule him; if he thought the shot in question was doubtful, he may allow a let; if he agreed with the Marker, he will allow that decision to stand. In the event of his overruling the Marker, there can be complications. He must really be absolutely certain that he saw very clearly what happened, and perhaps assume that the Marker had been unsighted, because otherwise he is awarding a rally with only his view to contradict the Marker's. Similarly, he must be very certain indeed, to stop a rally that the Marker is allowing to go on, that a shot was wrong. Nevertheless, if he is certain, then he would be acting contrary to the basic idea of getting the right result to the rally, if he did not rule accordingly. One point to beware of; if the Marker has called a ball out or not up, and the Referee rules that it was good, it is very rare that he can allow that shot to be a winner, and will probably allow a let. The reason is that, if the Marker had not called 'Out' or 'Not up', the opponent might well have got to the ball and returned it; the Referee could only interpret it as a winner if the opponent had absolutely no chance whatever of getting it anyway.

The other common appeal against the Marker's calls is when one player, or both, think that he has got the score wrong. This is why it is absolutely essential for both officials to write the score down; the Marker must do so because he has to keep calling it, and in a long and complex rally ought to be able to concentrate on the play without having to worry about the score and the side from which Hand in served, and the Referee must do so in order to be able to answer any appeal against the call. It is surprising how a question can create doubts in one's mind, however sure one thought one was, and written evidence is a great comfort, and the only way to be sure exactly what the score and side situation was at the start of the rally.

My own way or writing down the score is to make two columns headed by the names of the two players. At the end of each rally, I cross out the previous score, and put in the column, headed by the name of Hand in for the next rally, the score as it then is, followed by R or L to denote the side from which he serves. This method is economical in the use of paper and can be done on any old envelope or diary that is handy. I am rootedly opposed to printed score cards; not only can one not always guarantee to have one available, but lighting in a Squash court gallery, and the time available between rallies, make the inserting of figures into little printed squares a hazardous procedure. Also, a squash game may consist of nine rallies, or a vast number, and no card can cater for both; either a lot of card is going to be wasted, or one is going to need a large pile of cards! Apart from which, there is the quite unnecessary cost of printing them.

There are just two very important points to remember about writing down the score; one is that you must remember to cross out the previous score each time, so that there is only the one line to indicate the score, and not two to choose from, and secondly, it is vital for the Marker to write down the score before calling it. Otherwise, his call of the score will give the all clear for Hand in to serve, as always, and he is quite liable to do so while the Marker is looking down to write, and will thus miss a vital double fault.

So much for the normal duties of the Referee, but he is also in full charge of any untoward happenings, and must make sure no sharp practice of any kind occurs. He must make sure that there is no dangerous racket swinging, no barging or any other behaviour that could result in injury, no time wasting, no illegal leaving of the court during a game, no undesirable language, no arguing with his own decisions and no distracting behaviour that could put an opponent off. To cope with such situations, he has full power to deal with them as he thinks fit; he can warn, he can award lets or points, and in extreme or repeated cases, he may disqualify a player and award the match to his opponent. It is essential for the good of the game that he uses these powers wisely and well!

9. *Match Tactics*

At the beginning of Chapter Five, I explained that there were two sorts of tactics in squash, and proceeded to talk about elementary tactics, which are the basic things, which are always right in any game of squash. I now want to go on to match tactics, which vary from game to game. Previously I was pointing out, for example, that it is always correct, and indeed essential, for a player to return to the 'T' after every shot, but now we have come to the point where a particular tactic is only right in certain circumstances. What is right against one opponent on a low-roofed court with a fast ball may be suicide against a different opponent on a high-roofed court with a slow ball.

So, first of all, I want to discuss what these variables are that affect your decisions as to what style of play to adopt on that occasion, and indeed what shot to play each time you approach the ball. Because a squash racket is light, and the ball easy to hit, most competent players can play all the shots reasonably well, and provided two opponents are of approximately equal fitness, the one who will win will be the one who uses his repertoire of shots most effectively. This means sensible planning before the game, good use of the knock up, quick thinking during each rally and the ability to vary one's tactics as the game progresses.

The various things to be taken into consideration are the court on which the match is to be played, the opponent one is playing against, the ball one is using, the temperature in the court, which affects the behaviour of the ball, and one's own form and fitness. Let us look at these in detail, so that we can see the sort of thing that should be considered, before the match actually starts, bearing in mind that the pre-match plan has to be modified by information gained during the knock-up, and as the match goes on.

THE COURT

First, the court. I think we can assume that most match courts nowadays conform to the measurements laid down in the rules of the game, although some clubs do still play on some rather eccentric courts. However, even if the measurements are right, courts vary a great deal in other ways; the height of the roof, the type of lighting, and the brightness of it, the colour of the floor and the tin, the cleanness, or the reverse, of the walls, the position of the door, the construction of the walls, the existence of glass panels and any local peculiarities, such as bad cracks in the plaster, uneven flooring, protruding boards above the tin or along the out of court line, gaps between wall and floor or door hinges, and handles not flush with the wall. All these things will affect the play, and should be noted and assessed before the game starts. There are two reasons for this: firstly because it is necessary to work out in advance which shots are likely to be effective, and gear one's mind towards selecting these and discarding the alternatives; and secondly because so much of the winning of any game in any sport is confidence and concentration. If you have not given your mind the chance in advance of 'digesting' information about a court, you will have to do it during the knock up and the first game of the actual match, when you will have plenty of other things to think about, and things you could not consider before play actually began.

If the court roof is high, and none of the lights, beams or rafters are dangling low, then clearly it will be safe to use the lob service and the lob during the rallies. It will not only be safe to do so, but an even better idea than usual. if the background to this high ceiling is either very dark, very broken up or the lighting is poor. In some courts, squash is played in a part of a much larger building, with a dark ceiling a long way above the lights. This provides a background against which it is quite impossible to see a small black ball, and any overhead volley is a thoroughly chancy affair. On such a court, the lob is a 'must'. The obvious second point about playing under these conditions is that you should let the ball bounce whenever your opponent lobs you, rather than attempt a high volley by 'radar'. It is also difficult to pick up a high ball against a 'fussy' background of beams, rafters, struts, wires, panes of glass and so on. The ball appears to be flying very jerkily, and it is only too easy to mistime the shot.

Obviously lighting plays an important part, and combined with a uniform light background in the roof, bright fluorescent strips provide the best conditions for sighting the ball. These should ideally be situated so that the front pair are thrown on to the front wall, to provide the maximum illumination on the playing surface, but shielded from the players, and the two rear pairs slung parallel to the side walls. In this way, not only do they provide maximum and uniform lighting of the side walls, but an easier background, for the reason that it is less difficult to sight a ball coming down a line of light than going across it. All this should be taken into consideration when assessing a court and deciding how best to set your opponent problems, and what difficulties you are likely to experience yourself.

The next thing that will affect one's sight of the ball is the colour of the floor. The perfect colour is that of matched white Canadian maple strips, but many courts are far from perfect. The two most frequent snags are badly discoloured floors with engrimed dirt or stains, against which it is not easy to pick up a fast, low drive, or floors with different coloured strips, some the correct 'white' colour and the others varying shades of darker brown. This gives the same 'jerky' appearance to the flight of the ball as the broken-up ceiling background. Similarly, if the tin is not a light colour, it will provide a poor background for the hard-hit stroke.

While on the subject of the floor, another very vital aspect is worth noting before the game starts. All too many floors are 'oversealed', with a result that the surface is highly dangerous when any moisture gets on it. This does not mean merely when the court begins 'sweating', with condensation on the walls, as a result of which moisture is transferred by the ball on to the floor, though of course this does make for very treacherous conditions. It can happen much more frequently on otherwise dry courts when the players begin to sweat fairly heavily. The drops land on the highly glossy surface, cannot sink into it and be absorbed, and are spread over it to provide a lethal 'ice rink' effect. So before the match, note just how shiny the floor is and be prepared for a dangerously slippery surface, if it has got this highly polished look.

The walls, too, are important. Obviously the newer and cleaner they are, the better the background against which to see the ball; if they have been painted, and it is an 'outside' court in a cold spell, they will be liable to 'sweat', and provide conditions in which normal squash is ruled out. Normally, courts inside a building with walls not on the outside of it, are not likely to suffer, and of course, centrally-heated courts never do, whether the walls are painted or not. Ideally, it is desirable not to paint the walls, as this increases the tendency to sweating, as it seals up the natural porosity of the plaster, but there comes a time when walls can no longer be cleaned to a satisfactory colour, and the risk has to be taken. Because one's play has to be so radically different in 'condensation conditions', it is as well to have a good look at a court before a match, and assess the chances of these developing in your spell on the court.

The reason why tactics have to be so different is because the ball behaves so differently when striking a wet surface.

Normally, it will leave the wall at the same angle as when it approached it, but when there is moisture on the walls, it simply skids along it. Nor does it do even this consistently, but makes taking the ball off a wall a highly hazardous business. Two shots are ruled out at once : the lob, service or otherwise, simply continues its upward path on the front wall, and disappears into the roof; and any angle shot skids down the side wall, and instead of travelling across court, hits the front wall and rebounds to the 'T' for prompt despatch by the opponent. It is also risky to play any delicate shots after the ball has bounced; not only may it be carrying some water from contact with a wall, and thus skid on the floor, but it is also likely to be heavier than usual, and less easy to control for a 'touch' shot.

This narrows down the possibilities quite a bit, and the only way to play on a sweating court is to hit the ball hard and low all the time, and across court much more frequently than usual, for the very reason that it will skid down the side wall, rather than rebound normally, and this may defeat the opponent. The service is low over the cut line, and the only variety of stroke worth attempting is the volley drop, the 'stop' volley; the ball cannot misbehave in mid-air, and the opponent is probably so used to the barrage of hard drives that you have been producing, that a sudden shot into one of the front corners may well be a winner.

There is one other point about the walls which is worth considering. I was pointing out the advantages and dis-advantages of certain types of roof against which to see a high shot, but of course frequently, a player is watching the ball approaching, not against the roof, but against the part of the side wall between the out of court line and the roof. This may well be a continuation of the white wall, which is fine, but it may not. Sometimes the wall ceases at the line, and wire netting replaces it, preventing balls coming over from the next court. While the lights are on in that court, it is not too bad, but when they are not, it is a black and very difficult background, and if you are really unlucky, someone will actually turn the lights off just as you are watching the ball approaching! On other courts, the bare brickwork or some other less white surface continues above the line, and it is as well to register this before your match starts.

The height of the roof, lighting, floors and walls are the main things to check up on, but it is also useful to register any odd or unusual features about the court. It is better to do this, and have the information stored away in your mind, so that you can go on and concentrate on the knock up and the actual game, rather than come on court for the knock up and suddenly notice there is a glass back wall, or a door half way up one of the side walls, or a very bad patch of broken plaster in the centre of the front wall. It could then put you off, but would not do so, if you had known about it in advance. These things make little difference to your tactics, but it is as well to be prepared for the slight adjustments they may call for in individual shots, and not put off when some odd bounce occurs.

So do go and look at the court before your match, unless you already know it well, and store away all the relevant information.

YOUR OPPONENT

The next bit of research you need to do before the match is to find out all you can about your opponent, if you have neither seen him play, nor played him before. If you have run into him in the past, search the memory banks for all the bits of information you have stored away about his pet shots, speed and fitness, weaknesses, and so on. In either case, it helps if you can glean as much information about him as possible, before you go on court. You can usually find a friend who can tell you something about him, so listen and make some sort of plan, to be amended later when you actually see him, and even more, when you are knocking up. It is useful if you can discover, by hearsay, memory, or by studying his results, if there is any style of play against which he seems to be either very successful, or the reverse. If, for example, he seems to beat players you know to be good lob and drop men, but lose to those who are good runners, but never really go for shots, then it is clearly good sense to curb your shots, and stretch the rallies a bit.

Similarly, his appearance may give you a clue; it is dangerous to generalise, but on the whole certain types of strategy are more effective against certain types of opponent. For example, it is clearly easier to lob over the head of a short man, and it is more likely that your lobs will be cut off by a tall man. It is less difficult for a short man to turn and change direction quickly, whilst a tall man has the advantage of a long reach, but is suspect, when wrongfooted and made to turn. An older opponent may be very experienced, and have a wide range of shots, but is unlikely to relish long rallies, or being moved quickly about the court. Similarly, an opponent who is overweight, slightly injured or suffering from a bad cold, is unlikely to have the wind and stamina for a long match. On the other hand a young, fast, fit opponent may seek a long match, and the tactics against him might well be to slow him down by lobbing, so that the rallies are at your speed, not his, and win by frustrating him into errors, and playing winners as and when his efforts to speed things up lead to inaccurate shots back to the 'T'.

TEMPERATURE

So far we have discussed the court and the opponent, and about the only other thing that can be discovered before the match begins in earnest is the temperature. A squash ball is a piece of rubber surrounding a piece of air; when air is warmed up it expands, and when a rubber ball is expanded it becomes more bouncy and volatile. Thus, if a ball is heated up, either because the temperature is high or the players are warming it up by constant hard hitting, creating friction from their rackets, it will bound around the court to a far greater extent than a ball which is not being hit very hard in a match on a cold court in January. To try to get reasonably uniform behaviour, balls are manufactured in four speeds, with the idea that the 'fastest' should be used in the colder condition, and vice versa. However, any ball is responsive to temperature, and you can get a good idea of the speed at which your match will be played from the temperature in the court.

If conditions are going to be fast, then it will be more difficult to control drop shots, and more chance of lobs flying out of court; the ball will bounce higher off the floor and further from the walls, so that even if you take all the risks of playing a touch shot, and it works perfectly, the opponent still has plenty of time to get to the ball. You have, therefore, to resign yourself to long rallies, in which you take no risks, and only attempt winners when your opponent is a long way out of position. He still has to be moved around the court as much as possible, and the court is still longer than it is wide, so he must be made to run up and down rather than from side to side, but this should now be achieved by angles and drives to a length, rather than by using the riskier drops and lobs. An angle shot, though basically hit harder, will stay nearer to the front wall than a drop shot, because it is sliding across it and not striking it directly, and can be played perfectly safely. Thus, on a fast court, the accent is on the defensive service, length shots and angles, and winners have to be very definitely 'on' before the rewards, if they are successful, are worth the risk of them not being so! On a cold court it is much easier to make winners by good use of accurate lobs and drops, so the risk is far more worthwhile. However, it is equally easy for your opponent to attempt winners too, so although you should try to play an aggressive stroke every time the opportunity presents itself, in between times it is vital to play accurate defensive shots to a good length, and above all close to the side walls, to prevent him from having any openings for his winners.

PHYSICAL CONDITION

You have now learnt all you can about the external factors, which will affect the tactics to adopt in the match, so as you go to change, the last thing to consider is your own physical condition. If you are completely fit and feel sure you can last a long five game match, there is no need for any risky shots early; settle for long rallies and find out all you can about your opponent's strength and weaknesses, before attempting anything ambitious. After all, it would be a pity to lose 3–0 before your superior physical condition had had time to affect the result. If, however, you have been ill or injured, and are not fully fit, it is essential that you accept this, and do not embroil yourself in a long drawn out match, with hard slogging rallies; you will certainly lose if that happens, and your only chance of winning is to play twenty-seven winners before you collapse. If in attempting them, you hit twenty-seven down, you lose, but it is your only chance of winning, so you should have a go.

This does not mean taking ridiculous chances, but it does mean keeping the rallies reasonably slow, partly because it is less exhausting, and partly because the ball will remain slower, so that when the opportunity does present itself, your attempt at a winner is that much more likely to come off. If you can win by three games to love, so much the better, but if not, be prepared to take the risk of 'throwing' a game if necessary to conserve your strength for the next. For example, if you are a game or two up, but are 1–5 down in the next game, it would probably be wise to let it go, rather than risk exhausting yourself, and perhaps still lose it, and be in no state to make a really good start after the minute's rest. It is also quite off-putting to an opponent, when he knows he has been 'given' a game; he must feel he is up against some-one who is very confident, if he is prepared to let games go, and this does nothing for his own confidence. To do this, of course, it is necessary to be in the lead; the best situation is when you are two games up, know that you have the shots and speed to beat your opponent, provided the stamina holds out, but are tired at that moment. By walking around during the third game, simply lobbing, you can get the two periods of one minute each between games, plus the time it takes your opponent to win the third game, to recover, and have a real go at the fourth game. Of course, if the lobs happen to be particularly good, and you find you have an unexpected lead in the third game, you can always reconsider the situation, and try a spurt to see if in fact you can finish the match then and there.

Anyway, do bear in mind that it is a very useful tactic, when tired in a match, to expend the lead you have gained, or some of it, as a period for recharging the batteries. In the final of the 1971–2 Veterans' Championship I won the first two games fairly easily, but felt very tired. I could not have won the third even if I had tried, and if I had tried, would have been too tired to do much about the fourth or fifth games either. As it was, I 'threw' the third, and recovered enough to win a long fourth game; the scores of these two were 0–9, 10–9, and this is an excellent example of the value of this particular tactic.

KNOCKING UP

It is now time to go on court for the knock up. All the possible pre-match information has been duly registered, and has now to be checked, as far as possible, before the match actually starts. Is the court ceiling as good or bad a background as you thought? Is there any sign of condensation on the walls? Is your leg strain really better or does it feel as though it is going to give trouble, and so on? And now, although you have already thought about the temperature in the court, and whether the game will be fast or slow, you are actually using the match ball. You probably knew which type of ball it was going to be, that is to say which of the four speeds we mentioned earlier, but of course balls do vary somewhat from each other, even when they come out of the same box. The

E

knock up is the time during which you have to get the ball to its match speed and assess how its behaviour is going to affect your game, and which shots will be successful with it. It is also important to use the knock up to warm yourself up; it is very stupid to stand still until the match begins, and then start racing all over the court at full speed. That, particularly on a cold day, is the best way to pull muscles. Gradually get yourself loose and moving freely by moving up and down the court while knocking up, and if it is a more than usually freezing day, it is a good idea to do some warming-up exercises, before even going to the court.

The other thing to remember during the knock up is that when the match starts, you will aim to base yourself on the 'T'. It is not giving your eyes and reflexes much of a chance to prepare themselves for the match, if you knock up from well back in the court, and then suddenly expect them to react at the correct speed from several feet nearer the front wall. So, move around a good deal, but in general keep well up the court.

Then there is the question of what to practise; basically, you have two choices. Either you can try out all your shots, in order that you may discover which appear to be going well that day with that ball, or you can reveal nothing and simply hit the ball back to your opponent. The first idea has the advantage of getting your shots going, so that they are more likely to work when used in the match, but the disadvantage of revealing to the opponent that you can play these shots, and clearly intend to do so, or you would not be trying them out. The second conceals what shots you possess from your opponent, so that he does not know what to expect, but denies you the chance of getting them going, and as a result the first time you try them in the match, there is a risk that they may not work. Probably, the three factors which will help you decide are whether you have played the opponent before, whether you are in good practice, and whether you have played on that speed of court recently. In the first place, if you have played the particular opponent before, you will presumably have revealed your repertoire, so there is no point in not practising your shots; he knows them already, so make sure they are working well. Secondly, there is less need to practise them if you have been playing a lot, and they all seem to be in good order; but thirdly, even if you have been playing regularly, it may have been on a different type of court, and you may want to see how the shots are going with this faster or slower ball. Anyway, whatever you decide, do use the knock up sensibly, and do not, as so many players do, simply walk on the court and slam the ball around aimlessly.

In addition to concentrating on your own practice and warming up, take a good look at your opponent as well. Try to see if he has any obvious weaknesses or strengths; note what particular shots he seems to be trying out; test him with a lob or two, and a couple of hard drives straight at him, and try to judge his speed and footwork. Aim to add to, or amend, your initial ideas about him.

THE STATE OF THE MATCH

When the match starts in earnest, you should have a pretty good idea of what you intend to try, and how you aim to win. Whatever your basic tactics, it is vital to try to get a lead at the start of each game. This helps your own confidence and puts pressure on your opponent from the start. If you can get a lead of three or four points, you can afford then to take a few risks and attempt to play winners; if they do not work, you can cut them out for a while, and revert to the accurate, good length, risk-free type of game, in order to regain your lead. Nerves often play a part at the beginning of a match, and it is easy to snatch at the ball, or go for unearned winners through over-excitement or impatience; let your opponent do this, and present you with the points you need to get the whip hand in that game. It is also wise to start subsequent games the same way; usually the ball has been left lying on the floor after the previous game, and has had a minute to cool down. As a result, if you go for exactly the same perfect drop shot that won you the last point of the first game, at love all in the second, it is liable to go into the tin! So the first few rallies of each game are important, and the player, who uses his head and gets an early lead will have the initiative in that game, and has a good chance of going on to win it.

As the match progresses, so your ideas of how to go on to win it must also progress; if your initial tactics do not seem to be paying off, you must be ready to change them. You will often find that some of your initial premises were wrong, and thus the tactics you decided on, based on the assumption that they were right, must be altered. For instance, you may have thought, from the knock up, that your drop shot was going well, only to find that the first two you have tried have gone into the tin, so that shot has to be cut out for a while. Or you may have thought that your large opponent would be slow to turn, but in fact he appears to be a fully paid up ballet dancer. Also, conditions that were present at the start of the match have changed, and require that tactics are adjusted to the new situation. Walls which were dry at the start may now have begun to condense; the ball you began the match with has now broken, and its replacement is a good deal faster or slower; the leg injury you thought was better, so that you had quite happily gone along with fast rallies, is now playing up again, and you have to slow things down; you find that you suddenly appear much more or less fit than your opponent, contrary to expectation. So be prepared to think your way through a match; be alert to changing circumstances; be ready to try out new tactics like a prolonged spell of lobbing, a concentrated attack down his backhand wall, a sudden burst of hard low hitting, or a sudden slowing up of the game, or any other idea that you feel may disturb his rhythm and put him out of his stride. Remember it is better to go for winners when Hand in and to play that little bit more steadily when Hand out. Be aware of the score, and adapt your tactics to it.

After the match, remember that this has been just one in your squash career; do not be too elated if you have won, or too depressed if you have lost. The great thing is to learn something from each match, won or lost. You may have to play that opponent, or someone with a similar style, again on the same court, or one very like it, so do remember what went well and what did not, so that next time there will be less trial and error about your early tactics, and you may hit on the right things to do from the start. Remember that squash is chess played very fast, and what happens between the ears dictates what happens to the racket. Matches are won or lost in the minds of the players.

10. Fitness and Training for Squash

To be a champion at squash means combining a number of things. Up to a point, you have to have natural talent. There are some people who, through no fault of their own, will never be able to time a moving ball; others who cannot move quickly; and others whose reactions will never become quick enough to co-ordinate eye, footwork and racket. These are all physical considerations, and fortunately for such people, sport is now becoming so varied that there will be plenty of scope for them in other spheres, such as cycling, the field events in athletics, judo, gymnastics and so on. But squash demands a good eye, agility, a quick mind and very rapid reflexes. It also needs speed and stamina. The good eye, the quick mind and reflexes and the ability to move rapidly are gifts you are either born with or not; if you do not have them, you can never acquire them, and will never be more than a competent player of a ball game. If you do have them, they can be sharpened up by specialising on one particular activity, and this means playing, practising and thinking about that activity a very great deal. So it is with squash.

Squash, however, is a very physical game, and this is where speed and stamina come in. A player may have the most wonderful range of shots imaginable, but they are not going to be much use, if he is not fast enough about the court to get to the ball, and then play one of his superb winners. Similarly, a match at squash is normally the best of five games, and it comes to the same thing if you lose 0–3 or 2–3. So even if you are technically a far better player than your opponent, and lead by two games to love, it is not much use if you then fold up, because your lungs and legs have gone on strike, and he wins the next three games. So far I have tried to explain what a beginner can do to acquire the various shots, what the rules allow and require, how to practise strokes, and how to work out the correct strategy and tactics to beat an opponent. Now I have to try to make sure that you are fit enough to make use of all these winning shots and masterly tactics throughout the longest possible five game match.

WHAT TRAINING SUITS YOUR CIRCUMSTANCES?

This is not an easy task. This book will be read, in the main, by normal people doing normal full-time jobs, and not by the dedicated professional, who has nothing to do but train for, and play, squash. So some of the more exotic training programmes would be of little help. A bank clerk in Ashby-de-la-Zouch is not going to thank me for suggesting that he goes off and runs up and down Mount Kenya with Jonah Barrington, and an overweight schoolmaster in Bootle is unlikely to consider running through knee-deep surf on Bondi beach for miles each morning! So what training you do attempt for squash must be realisitic, and it depends largely on three things. Firstly, what your own circumstances are, secondly, what local facilities you have, and thirdly what time you are prepared to devote to training.

By 'your own circumstances' I mean things like your own physical make-up, your job and your type of mentality. For instance, if you are naturally slim and wiry, with no weight problem, you would be given different advice to a person who had to lose a couple of stone before he did anything else. So, too, would a person who had played top-class tennis or rugger, and was already fit for those sports, be given different advice to a middle-aged man who had just taken up squash after years of doing nothing more active than walking to and from the local. Jobs are important too. Someone doing outdoor work, such as a farmer, or market gardener, or an active person like a games master or Services P.T. instructor, would need a very different programme from that recommended for someone who sits at a desk all day working in artificial light and enjoying business lunches on the firm's expense account. One's mentality also comes in to this, because some people are able to stick to a routine, maintain their determination to work at something, and others are not: It is better to undertake something that one will be able to keep to, even if not very ambitious, than to embark on a highly demanding training programme and give it up after a week.

Then again it depends on your local facilities. It is not much use to anyone recommending a lot of gymnasium work, if there is no gymnasium for miles. On the other hand, if someone lives near a local rugger or soccer club, whose members train regularly, and are prepared to allow a guest to join in, this can be very helpful. Finally, the time element is important. Not everyone, for work or family reasons, can devote unlimited time to training. For many people, their available leisure time may be simply enough to keep their hand in at squash, without finding extra hours. Furthermore, not everyone is prepared to spend time in training, because they prefer actually playing squash, and I must admit that I have considerable sympathy with this point of view. I would certainly say that I believe that, for the vast majority of people, the maximum benefit from their available spare time can be obtained from actually playing squash, or practising it intelligently, and it is only someone, who is really intending to dedicate himself to the game, and is prepared to sacrifice other things to this end, who will profit from off-court activities. I will suggest some helpful ideas for these people in a moment.

Let me first of all stress why I feel as I do about practice on court. As I have tried to explain in earlier chapters, squash is a very intelligent game, chess played fast, if you like. It has a wide range of shots. These, practised hard and competitively, can provide most energetic training sessions. The very variety of the shots means that there will always be useful practice to be done on court, and only on court can one combine simultaneous training for the shots, moving about the court, thinking tactics, adapting oneself to the state of the game, acquiring stamina as required for squash and learning about different courts, balls and opponents. I am not saying that running round the block, circuit training, weights, springs and all the other training aids are not perfectly good in their own way, but what I am saying is that time on court should never be sacrified for some other form of fitness training, and any other activity should be carefully thought out and done, preferably under expert supervision, for a specific purpose.

Unintelligently done, such training can actively harm your squash prospects. For instance, I recall a very fine England player, who decided he wanted to improve his stamina by doing a lot of road running. After a while, his stamina and wind no doubt improved tremendously, but he found that he did not have just to run ten miles round a squash court, at long distance speed, he had to dart about, change direction and play shots all the time, and in every way, he found he had slowed down. Similarly, I well remember an overseas tourist who was a 'weights and springs' man; when he arrived in this country, he prided himself, rightly, on his strength and fitness. However, he found squash conditions very different here, with our colder courts, and he lost a few matches early on. Being a fitness fanatic, he could only conclude that he was not in peak condition, so he renewed and redoubled his efforts with the springs. The result was that he built up more and more muscle, became slower and slower, and lost more matches. What he needed to do, was to put a lot of time in on the English courts, get used to the bounce of the ball under these conditions, adapt his shots and realise what were the most dangerous strokes opponents would play at him; in other words, sort himself out on court.

Both these very fine players had concentrated on only one aspect of being fit for squash, and had in fact so overdone this, that the overall effect on their match results was disastrous. I am not saying that for the ordinary person, a bit of running early in September to work off the cricket season's beer paunch or some weight training to strengthen particular muscles atrophied by months behind the desk from 9 to 5, are not very good things. What I am saying is that they should be extras, over and above the maximum amount of time one can put in actually on a court.

KEEPING HEALTHY

Health, as opposed to fitness, is also tremendously important. However fit one is, a heavy cold, stomach upset, lack of sleep or hangover will all have a serious effect on your chances of beating someone at squash. This again is a topic where it is impossible to give specific advice. People's bodies vary enormously; some can do with five hours sleep per night, others need the full eight. Some people like to play a match immediately after a meal, because it allegedly gives them strength, and others like to have had nothing for several hours beforehand. Obviously, someone who does not drink or smoke is likely to be fitter than someone who does. Of the two, I view the occasional drinker as less unfit than the smoker. One can sweat the liquid out easier than one can 'unsoot' the lungs! Furthermore, and I think this is a very important point, it seems to be very much more difficult for someone who smokes a good deal to shake off a cold or cough, because his lungs are coated as a result of the smoke, and are therefore breeding grounds for germs, than for someone who does not smoke. As squash is a winter game, and catching the occasional cold in the English winter is unavoidable, it seems sense to me to do your best to ensure that any cold you do get is with you for the least possible time. You can only play considerably worse and feel miserable while you have it.

What I am trying to say is that anyone who wants to be fitter, and to play the game of squash more successfully and has the time at their disposal must try to do some training and become stronger, faster and more skilful. Each person must work out whether his own priority is on the fitness or the stroke playing side. As far as the state of that person's body is concerned, it is up to him (or her) to make sure it is as healthy as possible; he must make sure it gets geared to playing plenty of squash, and if ambition decrees, and time allows, he can improve his fitness in a number of ways especially geared to squash.

The word 'fit' is open to a lot of interpretations. If someone is asked how he is, and replies 'Pretty fit thanks', it means little more than that, at that moment, he has neither pneumonia nor appendicitis. But if a games player says he is 'not fit', it means he is not at what he knows to be his peak condition, and is probably not doing himself justice because of it.

Fitness itself is a very variable thing; a rugby international is presumably at his peak of strength and fitness for rugby football, but might be gasping helplessly for breath if asked to swim a couple of lengths of the local baths. A swimming star, who could do this with no trouble, might be quite exhausted after half a game of squash, and so on. Each sport makes its own demands; all top athletes and games players have built their particular specialised fitness on basic foundations of good health and sound physiques, but the specialised aspects vary considerably. To take an extreme case, a weight lifter would hardly need the same sort of preparation as a table tennis player. To me, fitness means being in the best possible condition to undertake the particular activity at which one is trying to excel. Any physical activity makes physical demands on the body, and if one is fit, one's rate of recovery from these demands is at its highest. What one has to decide is what the especial demands of squash are, and how one can best prepare one's body to meet them.

In a long and arduous match, the less fit player will find that he becomes out of breath, his legs get very weary and he may even feel sick. Any, or all, of these symptoms almost automatically reduces his will to win and determination to continue the battle at the same tempo. So stamina training is important, even though one hopes that an experienced player and tactician will be able to help himself in these crises by slowing the game down. Running, in some form, is obviously a basis for squash training, but not, in my view, merely long distance mileage. Squash type running may go on for quite a while, but it is in short, rapid darts around the court, seldom of more than a few yards, and frequently involving rapid changes of direction.

One of the best ways of training in this way is to go on to a court, and play rallies by yourself, playing the ball to the various corners of the court, and making a rule that you go there each time via the 'T'. This is creating the match type situation, brings in the exact type of running a match demands, means you are moving about carrying a racket, and playing strokes, and means, too, that you are having to get into position to play shots. In addition, because you are playing yourself, you can continue the rally as long as you want to, regardless of how often the ball bounces. If you do not have a court available when you want to train, you can presumably imitate this type of darting about in a garage or on any open space, though the facilities for combining running and racket skills would be lacking. If you do decide to run round the block, or on a track, try to intersperse short sprints with the merely mechanical, and even break into skipping or rapid leaps around a lamp-post occasionally!

One of the important things about any form of training is to combine it with a sensible way of life. However hard you train, you are going to sabotage all the good you might otherwise do if you continually stuff yourself with bread and potatoes, so that you are always overweight, or if you pour in half a dozen pints of beer after every session that might just have reduced the waist line, or if you always go to bed so late, that you are physically exhausted in the morning. Do not assume that a training programme is going to do it all for you unless you provide that programme with as healthy a body as possible to work on. One of the first things is to lose weight; partly because it is harder work, and therefore more tiring, to cart fourteen stone round a court than eleven, and secondly because fat acts as an insulator, and causes exhaustion from heat. I personally believe firmly in the theory that there are two types of food and drink which one can consume. The first are things which, if the body receives too much of them, it rejects and disposes of; the second, when more than sufficient are taken in, are stored as fat. In the first category go things like meat, fish, eggs and cheese, in the second go the breads, cakes, sweets, potatoes and so on. Within reason, fruit and salads and other vegetables are fine, but sugar in tea or coffee, drinks like tonic water, lemonade, beer, cider, wines and so on are definitely not. Whisky and water is probably the best for a slimmer who likes his drop of alcohol. Obviously restraint is the keynote, and there is a lot to be said for the old expression 'A little of what you fancy does you good'; the accent is on the 'little'.

EXERCISING AT HOME

For those who like to do exercises in their own houses, there are many which are helpful. All the well tried ones are of use, as learned in gym lessons at school, and many that are quoted in various squash magazines and publications. There are various types of skipping, running on the spot, jog trotting with sprints thrown in, hopping on one foot and so on. All are good if done to a pattern and plan, and help speed and agility, as well as strengthening leg muscles. The old hardy annuals, press-ups, are also very useful. The various permutations of lying on the back raising the legs slowly help with vital stomach muscles, or the legs can be moved up and down in a scissors movement. There are the various jumping exercises in which one can jump as high as possible, raising the knees as near the chest as possible with arms outstretched, and a recovery jump in between, or jumps astride and together, with arms alternately outstretched and brought together above the head.

Other useful exercises for the torso are from the sitting or lying position; with the hands clasped behind the neck, and elbows out, rise to a sitting position slowly, and when there, gradually circle forward to the right and left, or bend rapidly several times, forehead to alternate knees, before lying back again slowly. Then there are the exercises in which you stand with legs apart, and either touch your toes alternately with the opposite hands or stretch both hands together to the floor.

Any of these exercises, and many more, are of great help to anyone wishing to keep fit or strengthen any particular sets of muscles. As I tried to explain earlier, the needs of individuals vary so much that I cannot hope to suggest an infallible set of them which will suit everyone.

What one can do to make these exercises more effective is to work out a system whereby one goes through a certain routine. Having decided which particular exercises will be of the most use, devise a programme including a number of these; it is better to include a smaller number, and allow time for sufficient repetitions of each to get benefit from them, than try to do too many, and do each one twice only. This is known as 'circuit training', and it is easy to work out a very useful programme to suit your own needs and the time at your disposal. It is also a good way of disciplining oneself to do the same, or an increasing amount of work each day. It is ideally done in a gym.

For those who want to do weight training it is useful to remember that weights can be used in two ways: firstly, for increased strength, and secondly, to improve stamina. One can either build strength by lifting heavy weights occasionally, or stamina by lifting lighter weights often. They are designed on the 'overload' principle, in that one should try to increase the weights lifted a certain number of times, or increase the number of times the same weight is lifted. The theory is that speed and strength depend on each other, the stronger muscles a person has, the quicker that person can move his body into the correct position for a particular activity. There is some danger in a complete acceptance of this, as far as squash is concerned, because there is a risk that if certain muscles are over-developed, agility would be impaired, and speed for squash reduced; but by and large it is obviously good to have strong muscles.

The same profit can be gained from isometric exercises as from weights. These are easier to do in one way, in that you do not need any equipment, but use one part of the body itself as the 'weight' to exercise another. Very often a colleague can be useful to hold the feet or arms, and provide something against which to pull or push; in other words, these exercises are very much like the body pitting itself against the heaviness of weights, except that the resistance against which the body is working is now one's own hands or weight, or those of a friend. There are so many ways in which these can be devised, that I can do no more than outline the general idea here, but for example the wrist is a very vital link in the squash chain. This can be strengthened in two ways, very simply. Place one arm upwards along a table, bending the wrist upwards. Place the other hand against it, fingers facing fingers, pressing hard against each other. Or put the elbow on the table with the hand palm up and bent towards the shoulder. Press on the back of the hand with the other, and try to straighten the hand outwards.

You can also exercise the leg muscles used in jumping, turning and sudden acceleration in simple ways. Sit in an ordinary chair with your feet on the floor; raise your heels, and press down on the balls of your feet, and while doing so open and close the knees. To improve shoulder and arm muscles, stand with arms behind your back, right hand firmly gripped in the left; pull hard on each hand. Similarly, place the hands together, clasping each other, in front of the chest with elbows bent, and press the hands hard against each other. Then, linking the hands again in front of the chest, pull outwards hard. Maintain the effort in all these exercises for up to a quarter of a minute. Neck muscles can be strengthened by holding the palm of each hand in turn against the temple, and trying to turn the head to that side against the pressure of the hand. To exercise the muscles of the abdomen, sit on the floor with one knee at a time raised towards the chest. Put both hands, palms downwards, on the knee, and force it away from the body, while at the same time trying to bring it upwards towards the chest. Also for abdominal muscles, stand with knees slightly apart and half bent; put your hands on your knees, thumbs inside, and press down on the knees as hard as you can. For leg muscles, lie on your bed and loop a towel round your foot under the instep; bend the knee, and then try to extend the leg against the towel, which you held firmly in both hands, pulling towards you. You can also lie flat on the bed, with a pillow or cushion between your feet, and with your legs straight, press inwards and try to crush the cushion.

These exercises seem to me to cover most of the important muscle groups used in squash, and can be done very simply in one's own home with no apparatus at all; in fact quite a number can be done unobtrusively in the train on the way to work, or at the office, and in this way can be combined with maximum time on court, as they do not need special time devoted to them.

To sum up then : devote the maximum possible time to actual practice on court; do all you can to be healthy, rested and strong; work out training programmes which will suit your own physical needs and circumstances; and remember to develop the mind as well as the body, by thinking about the game.

11. Squash — A Survey

It is very much easier to quote established facts from the past than to forecast accurately the future. Nevertheless, in order to predict events to come, it is often wise to consider how the present situation has developed, and along which avenues in particular the 'floods' are spreading.

THE PAST . . .

The game began some hundred and thirty years ago, as an offshoot of the parent game of Rackets. The latter was, still is, and will remain a game played at certain public schools, wealthy clubs and universities. The reasons are largely economic rather than snobbish: a rackets court is a vast 'barn', which would cost many thousands of pounds to build in this day and age, and is too big a space to reserve for two people's sport, when it could be raking in large sums as storage space, or by being converted into offices. So it has remained a limited game played by a very few fortunate people, and can hardly ever aspire to be more than that. Its precocious child, squash, has long since outgrown the parent, but one of the main rasons for the recent 'avalanche' of courts and the truly tremendously rapid increase in the game's popularity in only a very few years, has been that it suddenly burst the class barrier and became a genuinely national sport in a way that rackets never could. It was suddenly brought to the notice of people who had never heard of it, at a time that coincided with a movement away from conventional team games; courts began to be available for everyone at a time when daily life was speeding up, and any physical exercise had to be fitted in to shorter periods in the ever more crowded working day. It fits into our climate – any game that can be played indoors in any weather and at any time of day must fit into our climate – but unlike the sedentary types of game such as like chess or bridge, squash provides the opportunity for fitness training and slimming, at a time when more and more people are becoming conscious of these things.

PRESENT . . .

Moving forward into the unaccustomed glare of press publicity, overseas tours, TV advertisements including squash rallies, and local court centres and clubs proclaiming their facilities, the game stands ready to spread itself in all directions. One film was made some years ago, not entirely successfully, of the final day of that year's Open Championship. Discussions have been going on ever since to create new films of general interest, as well as instructional films covering all angles of coaching. The TV companies are nibbling at the bait, and have already filmed some very limited extracts from matches. They remain, however, frightened by the technical difficulties involved in showing a very small ball, moving extremely quickly, probably against a not too clear background, with two large bodies in the way. Research into the problem has been very desultory, because TV has plenty of other sport to cover, and does not need squash. Squash, on the other hand, needs TV, and at some stage one hopes that the Squash Rackets Association technical experts can persuade the film men in TV that it is possible to show squash in a way that will enable the public to follow the ball, and persuade the authorities that squash would make an interesting change from show jumping, wrestling and motor sports!

. . . AND FUTURE

It is impossible to forecast the number of courts that will be built in the years ahead. Already the number being completed has far outstripped any forecasts of a few years ago, and there is every indication that this trend will continue. When the news reached this country that Japan was planning seven thousand courts in the next four years, everyone was overwhelmed. However, from current figures and development plans that I know of, I would be very surprised if Britain did not build more courts in the seventies than Japan, which, added to the existing ones, will give opportunities to everyone in the country to play. Squash courts seem to be 'virile' things; you stick up a couple in a new area and before you know where you are, another half dozen clubs have come into being. So far, I do not know of any area where saturation point has been reached. This may come, but I doubt it. Officially, when planners ask how many courts an area can take, the answer is one per 10,000 inhabitants. I personally believe it is nearer 1 to 1,000! My reasons for this are that squash can be played by men and women, and by the quite young and middle-aged, as well as those in their prime; thus anyone from ten to sixty is a likely candidate. Also, it can be combined with other sports, so that a rugger player, who would not be able to combine his rugger with hockey or soccer, can play squash, as can the hockey and soccer players.

Then there are the considerable number of people, who are members of several clubs for a number of reasons; they want to play in various competitions, they can get more games in this way, they want a club near their work as well as at home and so on. Furthermore, the keener the inhabitants of an area become, the more often they wish to play, and the more people there will be in that area 'exposed' to the lure of squash. Thus I believe that, as time goes on, more and more of the 1,000 people I mentioned will want to play squash, more of those who play will wish to play more often, and, particularly at peak periods, one court will not go far to satisfy the demand of this group!

So far, of course, squash has been almost entirely a participant, rather than a spectator, sport. Even those who do turn up and spectate at major events are invariably players, either past or present. Whether or not the game can expand to become any sort of major spectator attraction is still open to doubt. Clearly the successful development of glass walls leads one to wonder whether all four walls could be built of glass, and lit in such a way that the players could not see out, whilst the public could see in. This would enable a very considerable increase in spectators, as one could then arrange tier seating around all four walls. One would then have to discover what effect it would have on the nerves of the nearest row looking in through the front wall just above the tin, as the top players repeatedly drove the ball at them! I suppose it would be no worse than standing behind a cricket net as a fast bowler is letting fly, or being in the butts at Bisley, but, probably because I have got used to the other view, I think I will stick to the other end.

Seriously, however, we do not yet know whether all the possible positions would in fact be acceptable viewing situations, though I feel that the demand for the game is increasing so much, that it would result in people watching from anywhere for which they could buy tickets. Even so, the size of the ball and the speed at which it is hit must always militate against a vast crowd watching. The human eye would hardly see very much, from the back of one of Hampden Park's stands, of a game of squash played in a court erected in the middle of the field!

Maybe the answer would be to play in complete darkness, with all the lines on the floor and walls picked out in luminous paint, and a further strip around all the 'nicks' between walls, and walls and floors, and with the ball, rackets and players made fluorescent!

No, I think the maximum crowd that could ever hope to

see a squash match properly will be a very few thousand only, if that, and our hopes for spectators must lie with television.

NEW MATERIALS

Whilst on the topic of building, clearly there is still a vast amount of research to be done into better, cheaper, longer lasting and perhaps revolutionary methods of court construction. Even in the last few years, new types of wall surface have been approved, probably because of the continual difficulty in of finding a reliable plaster, and still more important, competent and conscientious plasterers to put it on the walls! I have always felt that builders have kept their prices high in order to cover themselves in case of a plaster failure requiring them to repair walls during the guarantee period! The precast concrete courts have been with us for some time now, and glass is no longer a novelty. More recently, compressed asbestos sheeting and fibre-glass have also been tried with success, and it may well be that some process such as this may lead to the perfect wall in due course.

There have also been many experiments with various types of flooring, methods of springing, and types of wood, and these continue. Whenever any new material appears and can be tested in court, the S.R.A. does so, and if the result is a satisfactory game, then that substance is 'approved'. In many cases, it may be some time before we can change the 'approved' into 'recommended'. After all, a governing body would be highly irresponsible if, purely as a result of one good game in a court, whose walls were finished with a new sort of plaster, they recommended this to all and sundry, only to find that within a year the plaster had crumbled to a fine powder. All that can be said, until time has proved the value of the new material, is that it is approved of for the present, and anyone wishing to use it must accept any risk of it not lasting. With the obvious potential demand for courts throughout this country and the world, much expertise in the building world will go into the problems of court construction in the future, and I am sure that in the end a better, safer and quicker method of supplying a playing surface than plaster will be found. I certainly hope so.

In the same way that I can see plaster becoming a thing of the past, I also hope in time that some substance can be found to replace rubber in the manufacture of squash balls. Plaster and rubber have proved my biggest and most recurring headaches as Technical Adviser of the S.R.A. since 1958. There has not been one season in which players have not complained about the ball; either it has been too fast, too dead, too 'squashy', too shiny or it has broken too often. More usually, each season has produced not one, but most, of these complaints! The advent of the Australian type ball was an improvement, and did lead to more uniformity, but rubber is a difficult and unpredictable material to work with, and until a synthetic ball, of completely forecastable behaviour, can be perfected, we shall continue to have complaints and comments about variability and breakages. Maybe, with the spread of the game to new countries where it was hitherto unknown, new technical minds will bring new thinking to squash, and we shall gain tremendously from this.

DIFFERENT TYPES OF CLUBS

Naturally, with all the building of courts that is going on in this country, a very wide range of clubs is emerging. At one end of the scale, there are the completely commercial centres, purely for the use of any member of the public who cares to go along and hire a court for a period. At the other end, there are the closed members' courts, available only to those who are individual members of the club or society concerned. In between are all the various permutations, such as municipal centres, commercially run clubs, centres with clubs attached, or at which clubs may 'block book', and so on. No doubt, all these various types of club will increase, and there will be a demand for all. Up to now, the big complexes have certainly provided the opportunity for thousands of people to be introduced to the game for the first time, and for these beginners to have a great deal of pleasure. They have not as yet produced any great players. Perhaps there are reasons for this; in the first place, few of these 'clubs' have very much in the way of facilities for coaching, and the financial angle is rather too much in the minds of those in charge to allow them to have very many league or competitive games. Thus any ambitious young player, who wants to get on, is forced to go off and join a members' type club, where there is a reputable coach, and where there are two or three teams playing in various competitions. As a result of this, of course, these clubs will have strong first and second team players, who are excellent opposition for promising youngsters on the way up, and whose matches at the club in home fixtures provide squash of a quality far beyond anything to be seen, and thus learned from, at the big centres.

Maybe these are the respective functions of the two main groups of clubs; the big centres will provide opportunities for those who have never played to get acquainted with the game, and for those who want to play casually and occasionally to do so without having to pay subscriptions and entrance fees. The hope is that, from time to time, from among the large number of beginners at these centres, there will be one or two able players who become bitten by the game and inspired to try and get somewhere at it.

COACHES AND COACHING

This leads on to the question of Coaches and Coaching. Early in the 1960s it became clear to the S.R.A. that a large number of people were beginning to take up the game. At that time, there were very few professional coaches, and the financial possibilities were not sufficient to attract young players to turn 'pro'. Thus, there was an ever-decreasing number of coaches, who were also becoming older year by year. The only newcomers were Egyptians or Pakistanis, who were all very competent players, but had two major drawbacks. In the first place, they were natural players themselves, and so found it very difficult to understand the problems of the rabbit, who simply could not hit the ball, or the person whose co-ordination and reflexes were less sharp than theirs. They also, on the whole, were unable to speak English well enough to explain their ideas comprehensibly, and thus their sole value was in improving the play, anticipation and fiftness of the already experienced players.

To try to remedy this dearth of coaches, the S.R.A. appointed a Director of Coaching, whose duty was to be to create a cadre of amateur coaches to fill this gap. I was lucky enough to be asked to do this job, and I have found it a very interesting and rewarding one.

Initially, I thought it best to provide a limited number of very highly qualified coaches, rather than flood the country with a whole host of indifferent ones, and I am sure this policy was right. We held week-end courses, usually at the Crystal Palace, for fifty volunteers, and examined them some months later. At the exam, they had to answer a written paper containing questions on the rules, refereeing and marking, tactics and organizing a coaching course. They were then tested practically on their ability to coach a beginner, to 'feed' a club player to allow him to practise particular strokes, to demonstrate all the shots and to spot faults. They were then required to mark and referee competently and to deliver a brief lecture on some topic of the game. Only around 50 per cent of candidates pass the exam, and of course not all members of the original fifty even attempted it, so it is tough and exacting road to the certificate. However, those who achieve it are authorities on the game and can feel confident that the instruction they give is sound, and above all consistent with that of other coaches.

Once sufficient of these coaches were spread around the country, it was possible to take the scheme to the next stage, which was the appointment of Area Coaching Representatives. These gentlemen were responsible for the coaching in their area, and to assist them, were encouraged to appoint County Coaching Representatives. Then, by using any available coaches in the county or area, it became possible to arrange courses for the 'second tier' coaches, leading to the Elementary Coaching Certificate. Initially, because the demands and standards of the various areas differed a great deal, there were 'area' certificates only, but after a few years, there had been considerable discussion over the content of these elementary courses, and methods of examining candidates, and a sufficient degree of uniformity became possible to make the certificate a national one. My ultimate aim was always to provide at least one elementary coach at every club, school, centre, etc., where squash was played, so that any beginner could be sure of good advice from the start, and this remains the aim. Now that a National Coach has been appointed, no doubt this scheme will accelerate, and one of his tasks will be to ensure uniformity in the instruction and examination of these lower level coaches throughout the country.

In order to make our coaching scheme work, we had somehow to persuade the authorities to allow qualified coaches to accept a fee. We wanted to make use of the expertise and teaching ability of people, who might otherwise have had to use their spare time supplementing their income in other ways, such as setting or marking academic papers. We were fortunate indeed to have as wise a person as Jack Giles at the helm of the Professionals S.R.A.; not only did he not view the scheme as a direct threat to the livelihood of his members, but was also far sighted enough to realise that such a scheme was for the good of the game, and could well be in the Professionals' own interests to have an ever-increasing number of people encouraged to play the game they taught. He has also been, from the very start, the instructor and chief examiner in the practical side of the scheme, and his contribution has been invaluable. Perhaps the greatest compliments the scheme can have are the continously increasing number of people coming forward for each course, and the fact that other countries are keen to develop similar schemes, and ask us to visit them to set these up.

REFEREES AND MARKERS

Another great shortage has always been in the Refereeing and Marking line. To try to combat this, the S.R.A. brought in another scheme for educating and examining people and awarding certificates. This also came under my 'umbrella' as Director of Coaching. The course was simply the same lectures on the Rules, Refereeing and Marking as given to the coaches, but the examination was more severe, and required a very much higher standard before the certificate was awarded. This scheme now continues on a wider and more 'frequent' basis with the help of the National Coach. Unfortunately, it will take time for this scheme to be fully successful. A coach may improve with experience, but he will be able to do a pretty good job from the time he is awarded his certificate, and any mistakes he makes will probably not be noticed by his class, who are likely to be learners. A Referee or Marker, on the other hand, must be in charge of a match, which means that the players are of at least a fairly competent standard. Any error or inconsistency on his part will be noticed at once, and there is more chance of this happening, because decisions have to be made at once, not after due planning, as for a coaching course! Also, any mistake may have a very serious effect; not only may any rally be the deciding rally in that game, and thus that match, but even if it is not, it may well have a very unsettling effect, not only on the player concerned, but also perhaps on his opponent, even though he has gained as a result. However able a player a person is or has been, however intelligent or quick witted he may be, only very frequent experience over a long period will make him a really efficient Marker and Referee. This is one of the reasons why we do not examine candidates at the actual course. It will be very clear when they appear for a subsequent examination whether or not they have put in the time and practice necessary, or whether they are just hoping for a lucky exam. If the exam were to be held immediately after the course, the person with a good memory might pass, and within weeks be a disaster, when asked to take charge of a match.

One of the things necessary to assist Markers and Referees is an international attempt to educate players, as well as the officials, in the rules, and to clamp down ruthlessly on any attempts to argue with decisions or show dissent. Players very often have never bothered to read the rules, and even sometimes pride themselves on the fact, and yet they are very ready to criticise a Marker who, in the pressure of a high-speed match, makes a call in a borderline situation, with which they disagree. In the main, Markers volunteer for the job, and one of the reasons why we are always so short of them is because only the very keenest will continue to offer to do a job for which they get few thanks, a lot of criticism and, only too frequently, are victims of loud and ill-mannered dissent from the players.

I believe the International Federation must ensure that the governing bodies of all member nations instruct their players in the rules, and make it very clear indeed that Referees' decisions are final, and comments of any sort from the court are inadmissible. I would like to see a system introduced, rather as in soccer, whereby Referees automatically report the name of any player showing dissent to the governing body in that country, and when three 'bookings' are chalked up against a player, he is automatically banned from tournament play for a period. This is undesirable, of course, but from observation of the court manners of a few leading players – and I do stress 'a few' – over the past fifteen years, I think it is necessary to counter the difficulty of persuading people to come forward to mark and Referee. It is obvious that the tension that causes these outbursts can only increase with the greater prize money now in the game, the frequency of attractive overseas tours for which there is great competition and the constant pressure of an ever growing number of competitions for both teams and individuals.

Similarly, I think the International Squash Rackets Federation must keep itself very much on the alert and ready to make any alterations in the rules, or more likely in the 'notes to Referees' on how to interpret them, in order to counter any new undesirable or unfair practices, that may appear from time to time as a result of this increased competitive pressure. I think it must always be remembered that there are two people with potentially lethal weapons in their hands, in a small area in which the mental atmosphere can become explosive. We must give the Referees of the future the power to cool these situations, or end them, before someone gets hurt, and the full backing of the associations, if they have taken drastic action. It can be argued that the power is there in the rules already, but when no Referee has actually ordered a player to 'leave the court' and awarded the match to his opponent for years, if ever, it is a brave man who does it for the first time. Yet it may be necessary, and it should be made clear that if it is, a Referee should not hesitate, and can feel sure of support.

PUT SOMETHING BACK

I think perhaps I would like to end this book with a plea to all those who get, or have got, enjoyment from the game of squash, to put something back into it. There will be an every increasing demand for coaches, for Referees and Markers and for people willing to help organise things at every level as the game grows. The current top players have too much on their plates already with constant match play, training and travel, and while they are at international level, one asks little more of them than that they should be a credit to the game and to themselves. But when they are no longer under such pressure one does look to them to use their reputation and influence to help the game along in some way. We are constantly looking for 'willing horses' at S.R.A. level and at county level, and I am sure very few clubs have all the helpers they could use, and that any player, however indifferent a performer he may be on court, can be invaluable if he is prepared to devote some time to the 'behind the scenes' activities.

It is a great game – let's keep it that way!

Index